JUST
DON'T
FALL

JUST DON'T FALL

A HILARIOUSLY TRUE STORY OF CHILDHOOD CANCER AND OLYMPIC GREATNESS

JOSH SUNDQUIST

VIKING

VIKING
An imprint of Penguin Random House LLC, New York

First published in the United States of America by Viking,
an imprint of Penguin Random House LLC, 2023

Visit us online at PenguinRandomHouse.com.

Library of Congress Cataloging-in-Publication Data is available.

ISBN 9780593621998

1st Printing

Printed in the United States of America

LSCH

Design by Opal Roengchai
Text set in Adobe Caslon Pro

To Dr. Dunsmore

and the entire team at UVA Children's Hospital

EDITOR'S NOTE

These are true stories.

Memoirs are based on, well, memories. So they're inherently skewed by point of view and reliant on reconstructed dialogue. That said, the author has adhered to the truth of his memories to the best of his ability. In some cases, chronology has been condensed or shifted for the sake of pacing.

JUST
DON'T
FALL

The physical therapist says she has one last idea that might stop the pain from the thousands of tiny needles that are still stabbing my left foot, even now after the doctor gave me as much medicine as a nine-year-old can get at one time. The nerves that go to your right foot and the nerves that go to your left foot are connected in your spinal cord, she tells me, so your brain doesn't always know which foot is which. I say that I can always tell my right from my left, but she says this is different and sometimes if one foot hurts and the other one gets a foot rub, the two signals cancel each other out.

So Mom sits on the end of my bed and puts my right foot in her lap. She starts by rubbing my toes. Her hands are cold. I shiver. But after she rubs my foot for a few minutes, her hands start to feel warm like the heating pad I used to put on my left leg. She rubs my toes and then moves down to the middle, where the arch is, and then down to my heel, kneading my foot like pizza dough, the kind with the dark brown whole wheat crust and spinach on top that she always makes—the kind that tastes terrible. We always ask her to make pizza with white crust and pepperonis because we don't mind about eating lots of fat and cholesterol and having heart attacks when we grow up, but she still makes her whole wheat crust and spinach-on-top pizza every week.

And today, in the hospital, when she rubs my foot like the whole wheat pizza dough, the needles stabbing my invisible foot start to disappear. First there are a thousand needles, then only a hundred, then just one or two, and then, for the first time since my leg was cut off, I have no pain at all. I fall asleep.

1

I have always been fast. I have never met any kid who is faster than me in a race if we race from my mailbox to their mailbox. That's why I'm good at soccer. But even though I've been practicing soccer with the other homeschool kids since I was six—three whole years now—there are no other homeschool teams to play against, so I've never played in a real game.

Then one Sunday morning I walk into Sunday school class and see Aaron, a homeschool friend who goes to my church, wearing green shorts, a matching jersey, and knee-high socks. I have on my white collared shirt and scratchy dress pants.

"I can't believe your parents let you wear that to church!" I say.

"Well, my travel soccer team has a game right after Sunday school," Aaron says. "And I won't have time to change clothes before it starts."

A *travel* soccer team! They play games . . . against other teams! They wear uniforms . . . to church! And homeschoolers are allowed to play!

As soon as Sunday school finishes, I run down all three flights of stairs to the hall outside adult Sunday school. I wait while the adults have a final prayer that lasts almost *three hours*, and then I jump in front of Mom as she walks out the door.

"Mommy!" I say. "Can I please, please, please play on a travel soccer team?"

She gives her standard response: "We'll have to think about it"—which really means "We'll have to think about reasons you can't do it," which really means "No."

But I want that uniform. I want those shiny shorts and bright socks to wear in games against other soccer teams in other cities around Virginia. I want it more than anything I have ever wanted. So I keep asking Mom.

This is one of the advantages of homeschooling. You are with your mom all day, every day, so if there's something you want, you can ask her over and over again. Of course, you don't want to ask her so much that she gets annoyed—just enough so she doesn't forget. That's why I only ask every fifteen minutes. I did this the time Luke took his first steps and Mom said that he had figured out how to walk because he'd seen us walking all the time. So I asked Mom, "If we all flew around in jet packs all the time, would Luke figure out how to fly?" She said no, he wouldn't, but I thought it would be really, really cool if Luke could learn how to fly, so I kept asking every fifteen minutes for several weeks, hoping she would say yes. But she never did.

The soccer-team question turns out differently than the jet-pack question, though. I ask Mom about the soccer team all week, and after just five days of asking every fifteen minutes—"No," "We'll think about it," "Maybe"—Mom agrees—"but you can't wear your uniform to church"—to let me play. Awesome! But try-outs aren't for a few weeks, so I will use those weeks to practice and get good. I will start tomorrow, on Saturday.

• • •

It's Saturday morning, and I just woke up. I look at my alarm clock: 7:03. I do a quick calculation: an hour and fifty-seven minutes left. Less than two hours. I feel something warm under my foot. I pull back the covers and see Mom's heating pad, the piece of fabric that heats up when you plug it into the wall. I've been using it for almost four months. I like to put it on my leg to help the growing pains when I am trying to go to sleep. *I must have rolled around and pushed it down to my foot while I was asleep.* I switch it off and climb down the ladder. Matthew, sleeping in the bottom bunk—he gets the bottom because he is seven and I am nine—feels the bed move and wakes up.

"Is it Saturday?" he whispers, like there are other people in the room who might wake up if he talks too loud.

"Yeah," I whisper back.

"Yessss!" he says, scrunching his eyes together and smiling so I can see the gap where his adult teeth haven't poked through yet. "Sweet cereal!" (*Thweetthereal.*)

Matthew jumps out of bed, but I am already halfway down the hall to the kitchen. I beat him there because I have always been fast, and when I stop running, I slide several inches on my socks across the kitchen floor. I see it on the table: Honey O's, which you will love if you like Honey Nut Cheerios, trademark General Mills. It contains nine essential vitamins and is a good source of—

But while I am still reading the box, Matthew grabs it off the table. He lifts it with two hands and shakes it over his bowl. A couple of Honey O's land in the bottom. *Plink, plink.* He shakes the box a few more times, and the cereal comes out like an avalanche into his bowl and pieces are rolling off the table and onto the floor.

"Awwww*wwwww*!" I say, which is what you say when you see someone break a rule and they are going to be in trouble. The "awwww" starts out in a low voice and then you get higher and higher until you are saying the "*wwwww*" part.

"Oops," Matthew says.

"That's more than a half bowl of sweet cereal!" I say. "I'm gonna tell Mom."

"No, please"—*pleath*—"don't tell Mom," he says. "Watch."

He grabs a fistful of Honey O's from the table and returns them to the box. Twelve more fistfuls, and now the bowl is only half-full, and the pieces from the table and on the floor are back in the box.

"There, see?" Matthew says.

7:34 a.m.

"An hour and twenty-six minutes left," I say.

"Yeah," Matthew says.

Saturday is the best day because you don't have to vacuum or wash clothes or mop or dust or sweep or shake out the rugs. We watch Saturday-morning cartoons instead—the old kind, like Bugs Bunny and Road Runner, because we are allowed to watch them even though we are not allowed to watch most things.

Our TV has a special machine in it that reads the CC (which stands for "closed-captioning") so it can substitute for bad words.

For example, if someone says a bad word like "butt," the machine replaces it with "toe," so people on our TV say things like "I want to kick your toe."

After cartoons, Matthew and I run down the hall and wait at the door until my watch reads nine o'clock exactly. Then we push it open so fast, it swings around on its hinges and slams against the wall. We run across the bedroom and jump on Dad.

"Wake up! Wake up!"

"It's Saturday morning, Daddy!"

Dad groans. "Uuuuuuuuuuuuuuuuuuuuuuuuuuuuuuuuuuh."

I always jump on his stomach when he starts groaning like this because it pushes all the air out of his lungs and sounds funny.

"Uuuuu—HUMPH!—uuuuuuh . . ."

We shake him until he opens his eyes.

"Come on, Dad. It's nine. You said we could wake you up now," I say. "We are going to play soccer together today, remember?"

"Yes, I know . . . okay, okay, I'm awake," he says.

"Daddy, guess what," Matthew says.

"What?" Dad asks.

"The sweet cereal is Honey O's!" Matthew says. He says it like *oath*.

After Dad and I practice soccer Saturday afternoon, Mom makes me take a shower. She always makes me take a shower when I get sweaty, even if I just took one the day before. So I take my shower, and Dad takes his, and then we all go out to Country Cookin, where the vegetable buffet is free for kids under ten and only $3.99 for adults unless they order steak.

"And for you, sir?" the waitress says to Dad.

Dad likes to read name tags so he can use people's names at least once in every sentence. "Well, Sheri," he says, "I'll have a six-ounce steak, please."

"How would you like that coo—"

"Paaaul," Mom interrupts.

She gives Dad the same frown she gives me when I finish my homeschool assignments for the day in twenty minutes and she knows I rushed through and probably made lots of mistakes on my math problems. The side of her lip sinks inside her left cheek, and she leans her head slightly in the same direction.

"Ummm, actually, Sheri," Dad says, "I will just go with the buffet tonight."

"Okay," Sheri says, stacking our menus. "I'll be right back with those waters."

Matthew asks why Dad didn't get a steak. Mom answers before Dad can.

"Well, we are trying to save money right now," she says.

"Do you mean there is going to be less money in the entertainment budget?"

"Maybe."

"But—no fair!"

"Yeah," I say. "No fair!"

"Why are we trying to save money?" Matthew asks.

"So we can have more savings."

"I know, but whyyyyyyyyy?"

Dad looks at Mom. "Now's a good time," he says.

She nods.

"Boys," Dad says, "we're going to move in a few months, and after we move, I'm not going to have a job anymore."

"Move! Where?"

"What about soccer?"

"Why won't you have a job?"

"Is there a travel soccer team where we're going?"

Matthew and I are asking the questions, and Luke starts crying in his high chair. Mom takes a deep breath and breathes it out.

"I'll go get him some food," she says.

Dad slides out of the booth to let her stand up, and then he sits back down and starts talking again.

"Pastor Smuland has asked me to come work for the church," Dad says.

"Why? Is he leaving?" Matthew asks.

"No, our church is getting so big, the elders think we need two pastors."

"And they want you to be the other one?"

"Uh-huh."

"So why do we have to move?"

"Well . . . to be a pastor, you have to go to seminary—do you boys know what seminary is? It's like a school for people who want to be pastors. So we're going to move to Florida for two years . . . so I can go to seminary there."

"Cool!" Matthew says. "Can we go to Disney World?"

"We can probably do that, maybe once."

"Yeeesss!" Matthew says. He reaches up his hand so I will give him a high five, but I am not sure whether I should give it to him because I don't want to go to Florida. All my friends like Aaron and the other homeschool boys from church are here, and I have known all of them my whole entire life, and we race against each other during homeschool potlucks. Every summer, when I have a birthday, I invite all the homeschool boys to our house for a sleepover. This year, since I will turn ten, Mom and Dad were going to let me invite ten boys. If I'm in Florida for my birthday, I probably won't even *know* ten boys I can invite. And the worst part about moving is that soccer tryouts are soon, so I will miss most of the season.

But maybe I should give Matthew a high five anyway because he is my very best friend, an even better friend than the homeschool boys because I have known him longer. So I lift my hand in front of his, but I do it slowly, like I am volunteering to be the one to wash the dishes after dinner.

"Well…" I say. "Can I play on a travel soccer team in Florida?"

"We'll have to think about it," Dad says.

The next day is Sunday and we go to church, like always. Soon, Dad will stand up front and give sermons. That's the only good thing about moving to Florida—when we come back to Harrisonburg and Dad is Pastor Sundquist, our whole family will become famous because he will tell stories about us in his sermons.

• • •

On Sunday night, I can't sleep because my leg hurts and I have the heating pad turned up to high and I still can't sleep. I sit on the top bunk, staring at the ceiling. I'm tired of thinking about soccer. I've thought about the uniform I want to wear, the goals I want to score, the position I want to play, and how much everyone in Sunday school will want to talk to me when they find out how good I am. I've thought about all those things at least three times already. So I try thinking about when I grow up and become a computer programmer. I'll program video games and know all the cheat codes because I made them myself. Thinking about this normally makes me feel happy but not tonight because I'm so tired and I can't sleep since my leg hurts and the heating pad doesn't help.

"Good morning," Mom says the next day.

I frown and don't say anything so she will know it's not a good morning.

"What's wrong?"

"I barely slept. It took *for-ev-er* to fall asleep," I say.

"I'm sorry, pumpkin. Were you worried about something?"

"No, it was the growing pains," I say.

"Did you try the heating pad?"

"Yes, but my skin gets so hot on my thigh, so sometimes I have to turn it off."

Mom squeezes her eyebrows together. "You always have it on your thigh?" she says.

"Yeah . . ."

"On both thighs?"

"No, just my left."

Mom starts talking faster. "Only your left leg? Your left thigh is the only place it hurts?"

"Yes, it's the only place that hurts. I told you that like *a century ago*."

"I don't think so."

"I did."

"I would've remembered."

"I told you."

"Okay, well, we are going to the doctor."

"Why?"

"To find out what is wrong with your leg."

"When?"

"Today. Right now."

2

I am getting an X-ray. I sit up on a cold, flat table while a lady who is dressed like a nurse but is not a nurse, who is actually an *X-ray technician*, adjusts a giant machine above me. The X-ray technician hands me a blanket—which is the heaviest blanket I've ever lifted—and tells me to lay it across my lap.

When we get home, the red light for the answering machine on the phone is blinking. "Hi, Linda, it's Mike," a voice says, a voice I can tell is Dr. Marsh's. I can tell it's Dr. Marsh's because I hear his voice every Sunday at church when he plays guitar and leads us in singing the songs. "I have the X-ray results back. Please call me as soon as you get this. We need to—"

Mom picks up the phone before the message is finished playing, and the tiny cassette tape inside makes a screeching noise as it jerks to a stop.

"Hi, this is Linda. Thanks for calling so soon . . . All right . . . Yes . . ."

She listens for a while. Then she opens her mouth to talk but doesn't say any words.

She closes her eyes and does it again.

Finally, words come out.

"But four of them—four of them thought it was benign? . . .

Okay, just a minute . . ." She looks at the calendar. "Ummm . . . yes . . . next Wednesday at two is . . . fine."

She crosses off "soccer" on the calendar and writes in "CAT scan."

Tryouts for the travel team are in a month. I can't miss homeschool soccer practice!

"But, *Mom!*" I say. "*Soccer!* I need to go to soccer practice."

I say this in a whisper so she will be able to hear Dr. Marsh on the phone at the same time as she listens to me. But she puts a finger over her lips to shush me.

"What do—what do you think it is, Mike?"

Mom is allowed to call him Mike since she is an adult. As soon as I turn eighteen, I will start calling him Mike, too. I can't wait to be eighteen because then I'll go to college and be allowed to stay up late and eat whatever pizza I want and call grown-ups by their first names.

"Mom? *Mom!* Can't I go to this cat thing another day?"

She slides her hand over the part of the phone where you put your mouth. "Joshua, wait, please," she says. "Yes, sorry, go on, Mike."

After she finishes talking to Dr. Marsh, she tells me that it might be very serious, but only two of the radiologists thought so, and there were six radiologists, so four of them thought it was benign.

"What's a radiologist?" I ask.

"A doctor who looks at X-rays."

"Well, what's a benign?"

"Benign. Not 'a benign.' It means not cancer."

"So . . . two people thought I have cancer?"

"Yes," Mom says. "But only two."

All I know about cancer is that Grandpa died from it. I don't want to die. So I don't want to have cancer. But four out of six radiologists thought it was benign. They had a vote, and cancer lost. I will be all right. I think.

On Wednesday I miss homeschool soccer practice, where we only practice but never play games against other teams or wear lime-green uniforms, but I still love going to it. I miss practice so I can go to my CAT scan. It is the worst day of my life because the whole time I just think about the soccer I am missing. It is even worse than the day that *used* to be the worst day of my life, which was the day Papa made me pick up rotten crab apples in the grass in his backyard *all day* and only paid me ten cents.

On Friday I go to another doctor, Dr. Blanco. He works at the University of Virginia Children's Hospital an hour away, and he is called a Pediatric Orthopedic Surgeon. Since all three of the words in his title have Greek roots, and those old languages are so important on something called the SATs, Mom wants me to try to figure out what they mean.

"Think about it," she says on the drive to see Dr. Blanco. "Or-thopedic. What does 'ortho' mean?"

"Ummm . . . I don't know."

"Think about it."

"Like 'orthodox,' maybe?"

"No . . . sound it out . . . orrrr-thooooo."

"I don't really know, Mom."

"How about . . . like . . . ba-ba-ba . . . ba . . . own?" she says.

"Oh—bone?" I say.

"That's right, bone!" she says. "He's a bone surgeon. You're so smart!"

Dr. Blanco the bone surgeon says that based on my X-ray he would like to do a needle biopsy. He will push a needle down through all the muscle in my leg—which is a lot of muscle; he noticed that about me as soon as I walked in today. I nod when he says this because I know I am very fast and practice soccer a lot and that's probably why I have a lot of muscle. He says the needle will take out a sample of my femur so he can look at it under a microscope. Then he will know whether my bone is benign or not.

"Don't worry about the needle," he says. "We'll give you medicine to put you to sleep."

"Will I have to swallow a pill? I can't swallow pills."

"No, you'll breathe anesthesia through a mask," Dr. Blanco says. "Or, if you want, you can get a shot that will make you feel very tired, and then we will put the mask on your face so you can breathe the anesthesia."

This is an easy decision.

"I hate needles."

"That's fine," he says. "You can just start breathing through the mask and you'll go right to sleep."

Breathing through the mask and going right to sleep is not normal because normally I lie in bed for an hour or two thinking about things before I fall asleep. If falling asleep is that different with anesthesia, I wonder if *being* asleep with anesthesia is also different.

"When you're asleep for surgery, do you have dreams?" I ask.

"Actually, under anesthesia, most people don't dream."

That is scary. I am afraid about how one second I will be falling asleep with a mask over my face, and the next second I will wake up, but that actually two hours will have passed in between those two seconds. On the drive home, Mom tries to tell me that this happens every night when I sleep, but no, I tell her, when I go to sleep at night, I have dreams. I know how long I have been sleeping from how many dreams I have. Sometimes I wake up and know exactly what time it is without even looking at the alarm clock.

But when I am asleep for my surgery, I won't know what time it is. My mind will be completely dark and blank and empty. Dad says that's what hell is like. It's not like people think, like with all the fire and demons. Hell is really just being alone, alone in an empty black space where you float by yourself with no other people or thoughts or sounds.

So surgery is like hell. Everything is black and empty, and you can't measure it or know what is going on in the hospital where your body is. Worst of all, you might die there, in that blackness, and all of a sudden God will take you to heaven, and you'll say, "What's going on? Why am I in heaven?"

And God will say, "Sorry, you died while you were having surgery."

And then you will be so mad at God—even though you aren't supposed to be mad at God—because you will have died without having time to say goodbye to anyone in your family or play on a travel soccer team or go to college or get old enough to call grown-ups by their first names. That's why I am afraid of surgery—because I might go to sleep and never wake up. I might bleed to death or something during the operation, but since I will be in the blackness of anesthesia, I won't even know it. And then, all of a sudden, I will be dead. That's the worst way to die.

But I wake up from the surgery. I wake up and Mom and Dad are standing there and I am not in heaven. I am still alive and I am still on Earth. I smile.

"Joshua, your leg is benign," Mom says. She hugs me, but she is very careful when she does since I just woke up from surgery.

"So what's wrong with my leg, then?" I ask.

"We still don't know," Mom says.

"Dr. Blanco wants to wait six weeks," Dad says. "Then he'll do some more tests."

"So the needle—the bone—it was just, like, normal?" I ask.

"Dr. Blanco found dead cells," Mom says, and then adds, "But no cancer."

Dead? Dead cells? Sounds bad.

So I ask, "What if it's some kind of cancer that just kills the cells and then moves on to someplace else in your body?"

"That's not what cancer does," Mom says.

"Are you sure?"

"Well, I've never heard of anything like that."

3

Since it turns out I don't have cancer in my leg, we drive four hours to visit Nana and Papa, who are Mom's mom and dad.

When we pull into the driveway at Nana and Papa's, I jump out first because I am closest to the sliding door. This gives me a head start in the race against Matthew. I need it, because my leg still hurts from the needle biopsy last week. Halfway between the driveway and the front steps, Matthew catches up, so I stick my arm out to block him. I can hold him behind me and still win the race to the door. Then I hear dogs barking. I look up and see two dogs, both bigger than Matthew and almost as big as me, running faster than I've ever seen dogs run. They are coming toward us across the neighbor's front lawn. *I don't have cancer*, I suddenly think. The dogs have teeth as long as my fingers, and as they run, drool flows through their teeth and spills off their gums. *I don't have cancer.* One of the dogs is looking at me. He is making eye contact with me, just like a person would, but his eyes look angry like Matthew's do when we are fighting. *I don't have cancer*, I think, my mind locking. *But I am going to get killed by a dog.*

I am too scared to run or talk or move. Matthew and I stand still on the sidewalk. I can't stop looking at that dog's eyes. I want to look away, but I can't because it keeps looking at me.

I feel a sharp pain in my neck—I am choking! I can't breathe!—and my body flies backward. I am hanging by my shirt collar, and Mom is swinging me behind her. With her other arm, she grabs Matthew. As she pulls us back, she steps forward, in between us and the dogs. And now *Mom* is going to die, right now, she is going to die! Then I hear a whistle, and the dogs stop running and drop their heads at Mom's feet. A man is running across the yard. He is the one whistling.

"Come on, boys," he says. The dogs stop and walk over to him.

"Sorry about that," the man says with a smile, like he is thinking, *Aren't dogs just the funniest animals?*

The drive home a few days later is terrible because my leg is hurting, aching deep down. It hurts even more than it did a few weeks ago. Mom says that we will go back to the doctor first thing tomorrow and try again to find out what is wrong with it, but I say that doesn't help me feel better now.

"This looks like a totally different leg," Dr. Blanco says as he hangs some X-rays in front of a light on the wall. "Whatever is in your femur, it's changed, a lot, in the past couple weeks."

Dr. Blanco is going to have to do a full biopsy, which means I will have surgery where he will cut open my leg and look at it. He thinks it's probably a bone infection, and if it is, he will cut out the whole infection while I am still asleep. Since it looks like a totally different leg it might be cancer after all, but probably not, probably it's a bone infection that he will cut out. The surgery to cut out the bone infection will take eight hours, and I will wake up in a body cast. The body cast means I won't be able to get out of bed for a few weeks, and it means I won't be able to play soccer for a few months, maybe a whole year.

So I decide I will use my year of recovering from the surgery to do push-ups and sit-ups in my bedroom, getting stronger. By the time the year is over, I will be able to do hundreds of push-ups without stopping, one right after the other, *boom-boom-boom-boom* and the coach will definitely want me to play on the travel soccer team because I'll be so strong.

For this operation, I tell Dr. Blanco I don't want to put on the anesthesia mask. When I had the first biopsy—when I just sat down on the operating table and put on the mask—there were a few seconds just before I fell all the way asleep when my muscles were not obeying my thoughts anymore. I could *see* what was happening—the doctor put his arms around me and laid me on the bed, saying I was doing great—but I couldn't feel anything. And I couldn't move. It was like my whole body was tied up with a bunch of ropes like I was kidnapped. It was very scary. So even though I hate needles, this time I will have a shot with medicine that will help my mind feel sleepy before my muscles stop obeying me.

The night before the operation, we go to Country Cookin for dinner. Anesthesia can make you throw up, so you can't eat anything for twelve hours before surgery to make sure your stomach is empty. Mom wants me to fill up at the All-U-Can-Eat Country Vegetable Bar so I will not be hungry in the morning. I eat three plates, but by the time we are sitting in a little room at the hospital the next morning, I am hungry again. A nurse finds us. She is carrying some tubes.

"Good morning, Joshua," she says. She wears the same clothes all the surgery nurses wear—a green V-neck shirt with matching pants. It's a uniform, I guess. And it's green. But not the kind of green uniform I want to wear.

"Hi," I say.

"How are you feeling?"

"Fine, how are you?"

"I'm . . . good, thanks," she says, picking up a piece of rubber that looks like a very thick rubber band that got cut so now it's a rubber string, not a band. "I'm going to put your IV in now, all right?"

"Okay."

She ties the rubber string around my left arm. I hope she notices how much of the string it takes to fit all the way around my bicep muscles. She tells me to make a fist and squeeze as hard as I can. I squeeze my hand while she wipes my arm with alcohol, which stings a little and then feels cold. My other hand is holding Mom's hand, and I try not to squeeze hers too tight.

"Are you ready?" the nurse asks.

I nod and close my eyes.

"One, two, three."

I feel a sharp pain like someone with very long fingernails has pinched my skin and then twisted it.

"It's all over, Joshua. You can relax your hand."

I open my eyes and see the needle sticking out of my arm. The needle is attached to a syringe, and the nurse is trying to pull blood into it.

"Need to make sure I hit a vein," she says.

But there's no blood.

"I'm really sorry. I'm gonna have to move the needle around just a little bit to try and find a vein."

The nurse grabs my elbow with one hand, holding it firmly against the table. With her other hand, she adjusts the needle underneath my skin the way you would if you were pushing a straw through a plastic lid to locate the last remaining sip of an excellent milkshake. She pulls it out a little bit, then changes the direction of the needle and pushes it all the way in, as far as it will go. Still no blood. She moves the syringe around in several small circles, and it feels like she is shredding the muscles in my arm. A few drops of blood finally flow into the tube. This turns the liquid inside the syringe from clear to cloudy orange, like orange juice mixed with water. She pulls at the syringe, but the blood stops coming.

"Let's . . . uh . . . try that again," she says, pulling the needle out of my arm and smiling briefly at Mom and Dad, who do not smile back. The hole left by the needle starts bleeding, and Mom looks at the nurse, and I can tell Mom is thinking, *Why couldn't you find that blood?* because I am thinking the same thing.

The nurse soaks up the blood with a piece of fluffy fabric and then pushes the needle back through my skin right beside the first hole without counting to three. I clench my teeth together and close my eyes because that is what people always do when they get stuck with needles. This time blood flows into her syringe. I realize that I have been holding my breath ever since the nurse started adjusting the needle, so I let out the air and then let go of Mom's hand. It's over.

The nurse gets another syringe and pushes its liquid into the IV.

"You are going to start feeling sleepy."

Mom gives me a kiss.

"I love you," she says.

Even though you can't have dreams under anesthesia, when I wake up I can tell the surgery did not take eight hours . . . I can just feel it . . . too short . . . and . . . no body cast! There was supposed to be a bone infection, and Dr. Blanco was going to take it out, and I was going to wake up with a body cast! But there's nothing on my leg other than bandages. What happened? Where is the cast?

"Sorry, I am going to need you to sit up."

A different nurse than the one who stabbed me with the needle is talking to me. She presses a button so my bed lifts me to a sitting position. It makes me dizzy. Then someone else rolls a giant machine over until it is touching my chest.

"We just need a quick lung X-ray," the nurse says.

"Wha—why? Where are my parents?"

"Just a quick lung X-ray," the nurse says.

She gives that same answer to every question, no matter what

I ask, so I stop asking questions. Then she lets the bed back down and I am dizzy again and the ceiling is blurry so I close my eyes.

"Joshua," Mom says. Dad and Mom are standing on the left side of my bed. Their eyes are red like they stayed up past their bedtime, like when there's a really good book you have to know the ending of that you are reading under the covers with your flashlight so you don't get in trouble.

Mom looks at Dad.

"Joshua," Dad says, "Dr. Blanco found cancer in your leg."

I have cancer?

I have . . . cancer.

I have cancer!

My life drops out from underneath me, and I am falling into blackness through a hole in the bed, but I can't drop off completely because my head and shoulders and chest are so heavy. *I have cancer.* The future—that line I have always seen in my mind that stretches out for eighty years into space and has photos along it like me playing on a soccer team and one of me watching Star Wars when I am allowed to on my twelfth birthday and becoming a computer programmer when I grow up—that line is gone now, and I am lying in a hospital bed. Now the hospital bed is the only thing that exists in the whole universe. *I have cancer. I am going to die.*

Suddenly, as I continue to feel myself falling backward into the universe, I feel a sharp pain in my neck—I am choking! I can't breathe!—then I snap back to reality and realize it's not pain at all. I open my eyes. Mom is hugging me around the neck.

"I'm so sorry, Joshua," she says. "I am so—I am so sorry. We didn't—I wish there was something—I could help—"

The only time Mom ever cries is when she is very tired and it seems like no one appreciates everything she does around here. But now she is crying about my cancer. She looks into my eyes and then at my face and my chest and my left leg, in bandages. She shakes her head and leans into Dad, who seems to be looking out the window even though there are no windows in this room.

Ewing's sarcoma is the kind of cancer I have in my leg and it moves like the Vikings in the Middle Ages. It doesn't stay in one place and grow there like normal cancer. Instead, it moves through your body from place to place, fighting and feeding wherever it lands, leaving only dead cells behind. That's why the first biopsy, the needle biopsy, only found dead cells, which made Dr. Blanco think it was an infection. But when he did the second biopsy, instead of just sticking in a big needle, he cut my leg open with a knife so he could look at more cells than he did the first time. That's why he found the place in my bone where the cancer had moved to. When he found cancer instead of an infection, he had to make a new plan with new doctors. Cancer doctors. No more long surgery to cut out the infection and put me in a body cast. The new plan was to wake me up early and do a chest X-ray and have Mom and Dad walk over to my bed to tell me I have cancer.

I know all this because Mom and Dad told me. But some

parents of children with cancer, they said, don't tell their children everything about their sickness. Some children don't even know they have cancer at all because their parents don't want to scare them. But Mom and Dad have promised to always tell me everything.

"Even if you find out I am going to die? Would you tell me that?"

"Yes . . . even if . . . you were going to die."

Before I had cancer, the only person I knew who had it was Grandpa, who was the dad of my dad. He died from the cancer when I was a little boy. After he died I remember I asked Dad what percent of people got cancer. I asked because I wanted to know how many more people I knew would die from it. Of course, it would be other people, not me. I would be part of the percent that did not get it because I did not smoke a pipe like Grandpa did.

So when I first woke up from that biopsy and Mom and Dad told me there was cancer in my leg, I was very surprised because cancer was something *other* people died from. Cancer was not supposed to happen to *me*. It was unfair because everyone else I knew was at home doing their homeschool or practicing soccer in their backyard and I was stuck in a hospital finding out I had cancer even though I have never smoked a pipe.

So some other boy will get the spot that should have been mine on the travel soccer team I was supposed to try out for this week. And that boy will get to keep playing soccer, but I will die of cancer. What a rip-off.

But then my parents tell me I have a 50 percent chance to live. Which is the same percent of getting it right if you pick heads or tails when you flip a coin to see who gets the ball first in a soccer game. That means half the people with my kind of cancer will die. Which is great news because at first I thought I was going to die, a hundred percent. But now I know I have a coin-flip chance of surviving.

I will have chemotherapy treatments that will fight the cancer, like special warriors who were sent in to help the villagers defend against the Vikings. I will have chemotherapy for one year. After that, we will hope the cancer is gone and that it doesn't come back.

My chemotherapy treatments will come through something called a Port-a-Cath in my chest, which will be like a permanent IV. I will have to have another operation to put in this Port-a-Cath.

"Another operation?"

"Yes, but hopefully this will be the last one."

"Don't they need to take it out when I am done with the chemotherapy?"

"Yes, you're right. I guess you will have two more operations."

And there's something else, something called Side Effects, which are bad things that can happen to you from the chemotherapy. If the special warriors accidentally broke some things in the town they were defending, or killed a few villagers with friendly fire from their crossbows, that would be Side Effects.

• • •

On the way to the hospital for the operation to install my port, I tell Mom and Dad I want to go back to breathing the anesthesia through the mask. I will never ever let someone put an IV in my arm again. They look at each other and then Dad says that's fine with them. We get to the hospital and then go back to sit in the room with curtains everywhere. The curtains hang from the ceiling to make little rooms where you can sit and wait with your parents.

A nurse comes into our curtain room.

"We are ready to take you back, Joshua," she says. I am on crutches now because of the cancer, so the nurse has a wheelchair for me. But the nurse is the same one who stabbed me with that needle and then sliced up the inside of my arm before my last operation. No way I am going to leave Mom and Dad and let her take me to the blackness in the operating room. I will not go anywhere with her. You are supposed to obey adults, and the nurse is an adult, but I will not listen to her. I hate her.

"Joshua, we need to go now, sweetheart," she says.

Sweetheart? You don't even know me. Don't try to talk like you're my mother.

I lean on Mom—my real mom, not a nurse who is trying to act like my mom so she can trick me into getting stabbed with needles—and wrap my arms around her waist and hold my hands together. It's the same trick I use in the summer when I am wrestling with Dad in the pool. He has never been able to get me off without Matthew's help because the only way to get my hands apart is to pull back each finger individually. That takes one hand for each finger, and I have ten fingers.

"Joshua?" the nurse says. "Do you want to get better? You want to get better, don't you? You need to have surgery so you can get better."

Do I want to get better? Really? What do I look like, a three-year-old?

"I'm not going with you."

"Joshua," Mom says, "maybe you—"

"NO!"

The nurse pulls on my wrists gently. "Let's go."

But I am not going anywhere. She pulls harder. My arms don't move.

"I'm sorry," she says to Mom, and then she pulls as hard as she can, but it's still not enough because I am very strong. "I will be right back," she says.

The nurse returns with a man, probably a doctor.

"Not too excited about the operation today, huh?" he says, drying off his hands with a paper towel.

"No, I don't want—any more—" I start to cry. I am trying not to because I am strong and very brave like Mom always says, but I can't help it, and the crying takes control of me.

The doctor and the nurse each grab one of my arms and pull on them, but they don't know about how they have to pull off my fingers one by one. Dad knows from wrestling in the pool in the summer, but he doesn't tell them. Now Mom is crying, too.

"We are going to have to give him a sedative," the doctor says.

"A shot? Does that mean he's giving me a shot?" I say. "No more shots!"

"He doesn't want the sedative," Dad says. "He wants to breathe through the mask."

"If he won't come with us, we have no choice," the doctor says. He turns to the nurse. "Get the IV."

"Okay."

The doctor puts on rubber gloves.

"Daddy, don't let them give me a shot!"

"You cannot give my son a shot!"

"Ma'am, will you please hold your son still?"

The nurse returns with another man who is very heavy looking and holds me against the chair.

"No! Do not give him a shot!"

"Sir, I'm sorry. We have no choice here."

The doctor pushes the needle into a small glass bottle and pulls its liquid into the syringe.

"Are you listening to me? He wants the mask!"

"Get away! I don't want a shot!"

I am screaming and kicking against the man who is holding me still.

"Hold still, young man!"

The doctor walks toward me, holding the syringe the way you hold a pencil. Then he puts his thumb on where the eraser would be so he is ready to push the medicine out.

Dad stands in front of him.

"No! *He wants the mask.*"

The doctor stops, facing my dad like when you are having a staring contest where you try not to blink. I am still crying very loudly, but no one else is talking.

"Fine!" the doctor says.

Dad nods. He won the staring contest. I will get the mask instead of the shot. Which is good, but even though it is good I am still crying so hard I can barely breathe. They wheel me back to the operating room and put the mask against my face and my eyelids fall and the world is black.

When I wake up, there is an IV in my arm. And my chest hurts where they put in the port. I want to go home now that the operation is done, but I have to have my first chemotherapy treatment. It will last for seven days. Mom has gone home because there is only space for one other person to sleep on the couch in my room and it's the weekend, so Dad will stay with me.

Once the chemotherapy begins, a nurse hangs something on my IV pump that looks like a big ziplock bag filled with water. The nurse says it's actually salt water like in the ocean. She says I need to have fluids flowing into my body through my port all the time. Otherwise the chemotherapy will get stuck in my bladder and cause bladder cancer.

The nurse says the fluids make me have to pee at least once an hour but we are not allowed to use the word "pee" in my family. We only say "urinate." The nurse says I shouldn't use the toilet since they need to test all my urine. So we save it all in plastic jugs. Every hour, all day, I sit up on the side of my bed and Dad holds the jug in place while I fill it up. The same that night.

"Dad," I say, in a whisper. *"Dad!"*

He wakes up, and we do it—side of the bed, hold jug, fill up.

Then he falls back asleep. But I don't. My leg hurts too much. Finally, at about three o'clock in the morning, a dream starts playing on the back of my eyelids—which is the place where you watch your dreams, like your own personal TV—but just then a nurse walks in with another ziplock bag.

"Sorry, did I wake you?" he says, hanging the bag on my IV pump.

"Not really," I say.

Dad wakes up. Since he's awake anyway, he helps me use the jug.

"Dad, my leg hurts so much!"

"I'm sorry, Joshua. Is there anything I can do?"

"No."

"Do you want more medicine?"

"No."

"Do you want anything?"

"I just want to die," I say quietly.

"What?"

"I wish I could just die so my leg wouldn't hurt anymore."

"No, you don't."

"Yes," I say. "I do."

Dad doesn't answer. He puts his lips together, then separates them again.

"Is it all right if I watch TV?" I ask.

Dad blinks, but it takes a long time, like his eyelids are in slow motion. He breathes out the way you do if you are blowing up a balloon.

Then he says, "If you want to."

And it's so awesome that he says I can watch TV if I want to because before I had cancer I never got to watch TV except for Saturday Morning Cartoons.

If you go to regular school instead of homeschool, cancer is kind of like a snow day. When it snows, kids I know from church who go to regular school get to skip school that day and just go sledding instead. Which I wish I could do but Mom still makes us do our school before we go outside and play in the snow. She always says it is better to be homeschooled because the other kids will have to go to school on a Saturday or on a day in the summer to make up for the snow day.

Some kids like me who spend so much time in the hospital because they have cancer just skip school for an entire year, like a snow year. Which is a great benefit of having cancer. But not for me because my mom is my teacher, so she brings my schoolbooks to the hospital with us. Just like when I am at home, every day I have to read a certain number of pages in each school subject book. The number of pages I have to read each day is a math problem: it is the total number of pages in that textbook divided by the number of days in the school year. When I have read that number of pages in each book and done any quizzes and checked my answers to the quizzes that were in those pages, I am finished with my school for the day. If I have questions about what I am supposed to learn I can ask Mom about them but mostly I just read the books by myself.

Different families have different ways of doing their homeschool, and so do different brothers in the same family. At home I do all my schoolwork at a desk in my closet, and I do not come out for breakfast until I have finished all my school. That way I can go outside and play the rest of the day. But Matthew likes to look at his toys and go eat snacks and sometimes does not finish all his schoolwork until dinnertime. So he does not get to go outside as early as I do.

In the hospital, school is the same, except I do not get to go outside and instead of sitting in my closet I do my school in my hospital bed. Sometimes I wish I could skip school for a year like other kids in the hospital, but Mom tells me they will be behind because they had cancer and will go to college a year late. So actually I am glad I am homeschooled so I don't have to wait an extra year to start going to college and have no bedtime and no rules.

The annoying part about chemotherapy is I am attached to an IV machine by a tube that is only about six feet long. The IV machine can wheel, but I can't push it because I use crutches. Also you can't wheel the machine outside the hospital because the nurses need to keep adding fluid bags. It would be nice if the tube attaching me to the machine was longer, like many miles long, so I could go to church or even go home while I was still getting chemotherapy. But it is only six feet long, so on Sunday morning I do not go to church.

A six-year-old Korean boy moves into the other bed in my room. His name is Johnny. He has cancer, too, but Dad says I am not ever supposed to talk about cancer with Johnny because his parents haven't told him he has it.

"How long has he had cancer?" I ask Dad.

"About two years."

"And they still haven't told him?"

"No, I guess not."

"Dad?"

"Yeah?"

"Thanks for . . . telling me."

Dad looks over at me.

"Of course, Joshua. We could never keep secrets from you."

That night Mom comes to the hospital and Dad goes home because he has to go to work Monday morning. Mom brings my schoolbooks, but on Monday she doesn't make me finish my normal amount of homeschool work. She says we will just do a light load this week. So I get done early and ask Mom if I can play Nintendo. She says I can—*yes!*—and she brings in the Nintendo machine that sits on a table with wheels so you can roll it into your hospital room. Which is another good thing about getting cancer since I have never been allowed to play video games before. While I play Mario—Johnny pulls back the curtain between our beds.

"Hi," he says.

"Hello there," Mom says.

Johnny carries a chair from his side of the room and puts it beside my bed. He sits in the chair and watches me play Nintendo. I ask him if he wants to play a turn but he shakes his head. So he just sits beside Mom and me and watches. He does the same thing all day the next day, too. He never talks. After Johnny goes back to his side of the room and Mom pulls the curtain so he can go to sleep, I whisper to her to ask why Johnny's mom or dad doesn't sleep on the couch beside his bed.

"Because they don't have enough money—they can't miss work," Mom says. She tells me they live in a *mobile home*.

"A mobile home? Like Nana and Papa?"

"No, Nana and Papa live in a regular house—they just use an RV when they're on vacation. Johnny's family lives in a mobile home all the time."

"Oh," I say. "Does he have brothers or sisters?"

"No."

"That's good."

"Why?"

"Because they probably wouldn't all fit in the mobile home."

The next morning, while I am working on my light load, the walls start blinking.

"A fire has been reported," a voice in the ceiling says. "Please evacuate."

"A fire has been reported," the voice says, again. "Please evacuate."

I close my books and start to get out of bed so we don't get burned up in the fire. Mom stands up, too, and walks over to my IV pump so she can push it for me during our evacuation. Then all of a sudden the fire alarm stops, which is good because I did not really want to have to get out of bed.

Then a nurse walks in with her hand on Johnny's shoulder.

"Don't you ever do that again," she tells him. "I am going to have to call your mommy."

The nurse leaves, and Mom follows her into the hallway.

Johnny sits down in his chair beside my bed. We look at each other, and we laugh. Then Mom comes back in and says stop laughing because that was not funny, so we cover our mouths, but laughs keep exploding through our hands.

When my week of chemo is finally over, a nurse comes to take the IV out of my port. I say goodbye to Johnny. Mom and I get in the car, and she drives us out of the parking deck. I look back up at the hospital. *Which window was my room?* I can't tell. All the windows look the same from down here.

4

Right beside Country Cookin is the Everything-Is-One-Dollar Store. That's where I buy my LA Looks hair gel. I get the red kind because it has Level Five Most Extreme Hold. I put on huge globs of gel every morning—Mom says it makes my hair look plastic—so that whenever I look in the mirror I will see that my hair looks perfect. I hope sometime I will be walking around at the mall and someone will come up to me and say, "Hi there, I saw you walking around here at the mall, and I think your hair looks perfect, and I hire models for the JCPenney advertisements you get in the newspaper, and would you like to be one of our models?" You never know when this might happen, and that's why I use a lot of gel.

But soon I won't have hair because the chemotherapy will make it all fall out. When I think about this, I think about chunks of gelled-together hair sliding out of the skin in my head and into my hand, staying perfectly stiff even when I hear it bounce off the bottom of an empty trash can. So I ask Mom to shave my hair so I don't have to watch it fall out. She does, and now when I look in the mirror in the bathroom I can see the large bump on my head that has always been covered by my hair. I look stupid. I don't want anyone to see me like this. I want to stay in my room for the whole year of chemotherapy so no one sees me.

Matthew says he doesn't want me to have to be the only one without any hair. He asks Mom to shave his head, too. One of the homeschool boys asks Matthew why his head is shaved, and Matthew tells him it's so I don't feel sad about losing my hair and the boy asks his mom if he can shave his head, too. Then lots of moms start calling our mom saying their boys want shaved heads to help me not feel sad. So we set up some stools in the backyard and invite everyone over to our house. Mom runs an extension cord into the backyard and plugs in the electric razor. Eighteen boys from homeschool and church come over. Mrs. Marsh, who is married to Dr. Marsh, helps give the haircuts. Her three boys are there and all shave their heads. Mrs. Marsh calls it the Chemo Cut.

A reporter from the newspaper wants to write a story about the head-shaving party, so that night after we have gotten all the hair off the grass and put it under the bushes so it can help them grow, the reporter talks to Dad, Mom, and me in the family room.

"That looks annoying," he says.

"What?" I ask.

"That! That brace on your leg!"

"Yeah, it is, a little bit."

"Well . . . are you getting used to walking on crutches?"

"I guess so."

"Let me ask you this: What did you think when you first found out you had cancer?"

"I thought I was going to die."

"What about now? Do you think you are going to beat this disease?"

"Yeah."

Then Mom tells the reporter about how many times God has saved my life. When I was one, I ate a poisonous plant. When I was two, I tumbled down a flight of stairs. When I was six, I climbed up the maple tree in the backyard to the height of a telephone pole, and then a branch broke, and I fell fifty feet to the ground. My only injury was a partial break of a bone in my left arm. God has a guardian angel working overtime to protect me, Mom says. He sure must have a special plan for my life.

The reporter asks me if I have always been so optimistic. Was I ever sad about having cancer?

"A little bit," I say.

"Just a little?" he asks.

"What about the first night you had chemotherapy?" Dad interrupts.

"What?" I say.

Don't talk about that, Dad! Don't! Stop!

"Don't you remember . . . the night when you first got your port put in your chest?"

"I don't think so."

This is very close to a lie, and I don't want to lie, because I am pretty sure I do know what Dad is talking about, but I also don't want the reporter to know about that night, because I want him to write nice things about me in the newspaper.

"You said that your leg hurt so much"—*no, no, no, don't tell the reporter*—"you wished you could die."

It makes me so mad that Dad tells the reporter about this conversation we had at three o'clock in the morning right after

I found out I had cancer when my leg was throbbing with pain.

"I did?" I say, pretending to be surprised, like I forgot about all that. Which is also very close to a lie, but at least I don't *say* I forgot, I just *act* like I forgot.

"Yes, you did."

I am mad that now the reporter knows I am not brave and inspiring like he thought I was before.

"Well . . . does it still hurt that much?" the reporter asks.

"No, after about two days of chemotherapy, it stopped hurting."

Now the reporter turns to look at Dad, to ask him a question. I do not turn to look at him because I am so mad at him for telling the reporter that I wanted to die.

"How has cancer changed your family?"

"It's changed everything," Dad says—Dad, the one who tells reporters about conversations that should be a secret. "We were actually planning to move to Florida so I could go to seminary this summer. But because of Jo—um, because of the cancer, we are staying here."

I look up from the floor, where I am sitting. I have been thinking about my cancer all the time recently, and I forgot about Dad's seminary. Florida! The move! But now we're not going? We're staying here? Great! I am very happy about this because I do not want to move. And I am also kind of glad Dad doesn't get to go to seminary even though he wanted to, because I am mad at him.

"'It's changed everything.'" The reporter repeats Dad's words, writing on his pad. He looks up. "Even your faith?"

"No," Dad says.

"Not even a little?"

"It has not shaken my faith."

"So after Joshua is done with chemotherapy—will you go to seminary then?"

"Well . . . I'll pray about it . . . but the most important thing right now is for me to keep my job so we can keep our health insurance," Dad says. "And even after he's done with the chemotherapy, if his cancer ever relapsed, or if he had major side effects—"

Luke comes in, wearing only a diaper and a T-shirt and walking in that funny way one-year-olds walk. He holds his little hand up in the reporter's face.

"Look!" Luke says.

There's a brown speck on his palm.

"Hey there little guy. What is that?"

"It's a splinter," Mom says. "He got it about two weeks ago. I just . . . haven't had the heart to take it out yet."

Something starts to leak from the bottom of Luke's diaper.

"Oh, Luke!" Mom says, lifting him and carrying him away, holding her arms straight out.

Before I got cancer, Mom was taking Luke across the state to doctor after doctor, hoping one of them could figure out why Luke had had diarrhea for almost an entire year or at least prescribe something that helped. But now she only has time to talk to *my* doctors. So Luke still has diarrhea.

The reporter asks a few more questions and then he leaves because it is time for bed. When it is time for bed in our family, we have a rule that you have to tell everyone that you love them, whether you mean it or not. Tonight when I tell Dad I love him I don't really mean it because I am still mad at him. But when I tell Matthew I love him I *do* really mean it because he shaved his head for me and that made eighteen other boys also shave their heads. Tonight I have the most love I have ever had for Matthew.

Two weeks later, I go back to the hospital for another round of chemotherapy. On the third morning I wake up and there is black dust on my pillowcase. I brush it off with the back of my hand and go back to sleep. But the next time I wake up, my pillowcase is covered with it. Then I realize it is the roots of my hair. Mom couldn't shave it close enough. My hair is still falling out.

I look at Mom. She is awake.

"I'm sorry," she says.

I try not to cry—I haven't cried since the doctors pulled me off Mom and took me to surgery—but I can't help it. I start crying, and tears and drool are running out of my eyes and nose and mouth. Mom sits in my bed and holds me and rocks me back and forth.

"Mom?" I ask once the crying has changed into quick little breaths. "Do you think—do you think if we all flew around in jet packs that Luke would figure out how to fly?"

She smiles at me.

"Yes, sweetheart, I think he would."

We go home two days later and I spend a whole week lying in bed because I am too tired to do anything. Then Mom and

Dad say that since I am on crutches, I don't have to wear dress clothes if I come to church on Sunday. In fact, I can wear anything I want to church! So Sunday is a great day. I decide to wear a T-shirt and my favorite pair of pants which are black and shiny and water resistant. I pull the pants on over my leg brace. I find my baseball hat with a cross on it. You aren't supposed to wear a hat to church but I think it's okay because this one has a cross on it.

Before we leave, Mom takes me into her bathroom and uses makeup to draw black lines where my eyebrows used to be.

"Do you think they look like real eyebrows?" I ask.

"Yes, I think so," she says.

"Are you sure?"

"Well, I did my best."

I smile and hug her.

But when I climb into the minivan, Matthew stares at me.

"Hey, what's wrong with your eyebrows?" he says.

I look at Mom and her face is sad because she knows she did not do a good job drawing my eyebrows. I run back inside as fast as I can on my crutches and stare at my reflection in Mom's bathroom mirror.

"Looks like real eyebrows, Mom?" I say.

There's no one in the house, so I yell.

"Real eyebrows, huh? Yeah, right!"

I scream and pound the sink with both of my fists. Then my fists hurt from hitting the sink, and I take a piece of toilet paper and wipe it over the fake eyebrows. Some of the makeup comes off. The rest just smears across my forehead. So I splash water from the sink onto my face, and I get more sheets of toilet paper and rub them on my forehead until little balls of dark, wet toilet paper start falling in the sink.

At church, I have to walk up all three flights of stairs on my crutches, so I am late getting to Sunday school. But when I walk in wearing my black shiny pants over top of my leg brace and my backward hat with a cross on it, everyone claps. Several of them are the homeschool boys who shaved their heads for me—but I notice today that no one shaved their eyebrows for me.

I glance at Aaron. *Soon I'll finish the chemotherapy and get a soccer uniform like his.*

On Monday I am lying on the couch watching a Zorro movie that I am allowed to watch because it is in black-and-white. Mom comes in and sits beside me. She asks if I can pause it which I do not want to do because it is very exciting but I do anyway because Mom said so. Mom tells me that she got a call from Dr. Dunsmore, the lady who became my special doctor after I got cancer. The call was about Johnny, the little boy I shared a room with. Mom asks if I remember him.

"Yeah," I say.

"Well, he died yesterday."

"Really?"

I am not sure why I ask this because normally you say "Really?" only if you think the person is lying or joking, and Mom does not ever lie or tell jokes.

"Yes, really."

I think about how he was alive just a few weeks ago, and he sat beside me in the hospital, and he watched me play Nintendo and now I will never see him again.

"Would you like to go to the funeral?" Mom asks.

"Yes."

All that time when he sat beside me in the hospital, I never knew he would die and I would never see him again.

"You don't have to go if you don't want to."

"Okay."

"So do you still want to go?"

"Yes."

It is the first time I've ever been to a funeral. I don't ask Mom and Dad if I can wear a T-shirt and my shiny pants. I wear church clothes. After the service, people are drinking punch (it tastes like Hawaiian Punch, which is very good because it has a lot of sugar in it) and looking at photos of Johnny that are taped to pages in a big book. His mom is talking to my mom. Johnny's mom doesn't really speak English, and my mom doesn't speak any Korean, so their conversation is short.

While I drink punch, I wonder about a lot of things. I wonder if Johnny's mom is wishing she was my mom instead because then her son would not be dead. I wonder if Johnny's mom is still actually a mom at all since now she doesn't have any children who are alive. And I wonder if she is wishing she never had a son named Johnny because then he would not have died and she would not be at his sad funeral. This makes me hope that I die after Mom and Dad do. I do not want them to have to go to my funeral and wish they had never had me.

Then Johnny's mom turns to me and puts her hands on my cheeks.

"You such handsome boy!" she says and starts to cry. She puts her arms around me, but I don't hug her back. I just stand there, straight and stiff with my hands at my sides, because I'm mad Johnny never knew he had leukemia. He was six years old and had no idea his life was about to end even though all the grown-ups knew. The doctors gave him enough medicine that he was never in pain even though he was dying. Dr. Dunsmore told Mom that the day before Johnny died he started telling the nurses that he was getting ready to move out of his mobile home and into a big house.

"What big house?" they asked.

"The big house," he said. "It looks like a castle. It's right there."

And then he would point at the wall, or the sky, and the nurses would just nod at him because he was on so much pain medicine that he was seeing things that weren't really there. And even then his parents didn't tell him he was dying. Then—*poof*—the lights went out in his eyes and he was gone. Gone without a chance to say goodbye or build some blocks or draw another picture or whatever a six-year-old would want to do if he knew he was going to die.

This is the worst way to die. It's just like dying in the middle of an operation. You are there, and then you are not. At least if you are in a car wreck or fall off a tall building, you probably have a second or two to realize it's all about to end and you can choose a thought that you would like to be your final thought. But if you don't know it's coming there are no final thoughts. There are just thoughts, and then no thoughts. That's why I don't hug Johnny's mom. Because Johnny didn't get a final thought.

It's a month after Johnny's funeral, and we are driving home from Country Cookin. We don't go every week anymore since I am in the hospital so much and everyone is always tired. We just try to go when we can. As we drive the last block before our house I say how I can't wait until my leg is better so I can start playing soccer again.

"When will that be, do you think?" I ask.

Mom and Dad don't answer. They are sitting in the front seats of the van. I am behind them with Luke, who is sitting in his car seat beside me. Matthew is in the very back. Mom and Dad keep looking back at each other.

"So when can I get off the crutches?" I ask again as we pull into the driveway.

Dad puts the van in park and hands the keys to Matthew.

"Go inside," he says. "Take Luke with you."

Matthew unbuckles Luke and lifts him—Luke's getting really big, almost too heavy for Matthew to carry—to the driveway. They hold hands and walk up the sidewalk to the front door. We listen as keys jingle and then we hear the door open and then shut. And then we hear nothing.

"We need to talk to you about something," Dad says.

"Okay," I say.

Bad news is coming—that's why Dad gave Matthew the keys and told him to go inside. But how bad? Extra chemo treatments? Another surgery?

"The chemotherapy is not shrinking the tumor in your leg."

"Okay . . ."

Not shrinking? What does that mean? What happens when the cancer doesn't shrink?

"We have been talking to the doctors, and it's possible you— your leg might possibly have to be amputated."

I gag, choking on the air in the van. I know what an amputation is, but I can't believe it—no soccer! No running!—so I pretend like I don't understand.

"What does that mean?"

"It would mean . . . the doctors would cut off your leg."

"I don't want them to cut my leg off!"

I bend forward and wrap my arms around my leg. Tears drip onto my pants.

"I'm sorry Joshua," Dad says. "I wish they could amputate mine instead."

"How soon?" I ask.

"A few weeks, maybe."

After I stop crying it's quiet in the van. Usually when my brain remembers sounds they are things you can hear like music I listened to or words someone said to me. But even though quiet is not actually a sound this quiet in the van is so loud that I think I will always be able to remember it in my brain.

• • •

Each night while I lie on the bottom bunk—Matthew and I switched since I have to wear the leg brace and I can't climb up the ladder—I think about how my leg might possibly have to be amputated in a few weeks maybe, and I cry until I fall asleep. If I have one leg, I won't be able to do anything. I will have to sit in a chair all day and watch Matthew out the window while he plays soccer in the backyard. I try to cry softly so Matthew can't hear it, but probably he can because sometimes Dad hears and comes in and rubs my back.

We drive to Baltimore to meet an orthopedic surgeon at Johns Hopkins who will give us his opinion, which is called a second opinion since we already got a first opinion from Dr. Dunsmore. The Johns Hopkins doctor says his second opinion is that I need to do something to get rid of the cancer, but it does not have to be an amputation. *I could keep my leg?* He says he could take out my femur bone with the cancer in it and replace it with a metal rod. It would save my leg, but every six months I would have to have another operation to lengthen the rod to match my normal growth.

"So, if I still had my leg, I could play soccer, right?"

"Actually, no, not really. You wouldn't be able to run. Your leg would be too fragile."

"Could I play any sports?"

"You could do things where you stand in one place, like shooting baskets with your friends."

But standing in one place and shooting baskets is not a sport.

He has other ideas. He could replace my bone with a bone from someone who just died. But even though Johnny just died, I couldn't use Johnny's bone because they have to have died like in the last day and also they need to have been healthy and died in a car wreck instead of cancer. So that way you know their bones are healthy. It would be weird to have a piece of a dead person I never even met inside me but I would be all right if that means I could play sports. But the doctor says the dead person's bone would be just as fragile as a metal bone. No sports. He could also take out my femur and move my lower leg bone up, sewing my knee to my hip, with the foot turned around backward. This would allow me to keep half a leg instead of losing the whole thing.

"Wouldn't that look kind of . . . weird?"

"Yes, well, it is somewhat strange," he replies. "But it's very popular in Europe."

I have never been to Europe. I try to imagine a place where short legs with backward feet are popular.

The surgeon says my only other option is amputation, which is my best chance at living.

"With an amputation, you will have a harder time getting around in life, but I would not tell you you're not allowed to run or play sports," the surgeon says. "In fact, I know amputees who ride bikes, swim, ski, even a few who play soccer."

"Really? Amputees play soccer?"

"Well, yes, but they are a lower level than you would be," he says. "These are people who only lost their foot. You would lose your whole leg from the hip."

"But I could play sports if I wanted to?"

"Sure, you could try."

For the first time since that conversation in the van with my parents it seems like there may be a good reason to keep fighting the cancer: I can play sports again. I can become fast again. I can be free and I can be fast. Free, because I would no longer be weighed down by the feeling that something inside my body wants to kill me. Fast, because I could do push-ups one right after the other until I got strong again. Then I would get a uniform, a uniform with matching socks and shorts and a shirt, and I would wear it to church every single Sunday over top of my fake leg and no one could tell me that I can't wear it on Sunday and every day of the week, too, because I would be a cancer survivor who is free. So now I know. I have to survive. I have to live. I have to get that uniform.

5

The night before the operation we do not go to Country Cookin even though I know I'll be hungry in the morning. I don't feel like going anywhere or seeing any people.

The next morning as we drive over the mountain to the hospital I sit in the back of the van and listen to the engine. *Huuuummmmm.* I lean my head against the window and feel it vibrate on my forehead. I look at the people in the other cars and wonder what they are doing today. Probably going to work or to the grocery store or something. I wish I was one of them. Any of them.

In the hospital we wait in a little space with some chairs surrounded by a curtain hanging from the ceiling. I take off the leg brace I've worn for three months and lay it on the floor because I won't need to wear it anymore. Then I bend over and wrap both arms around my leg. I sit like that for a long time and it is very quiet. *I will wake up and my leg will be gone.* Then a nurse comes in and asks me to put on a hospital gown and a pair of brown socks that are made out of fabric like a towel and have rubber strips on the bottom to help you grip the floor. *My leg will be gone, but I will still be here. I will survive.* A few minutes later she returns with a doctor and an empty wheelchair and the fat man who held me down before my last surgery. *I will beat the cancer. I will learn how to run. I will be strong.* The fat man walks over and stands beside me. The doctor looks at my parents and they nod.

"Joshua, can we take you to the operating room now?" the doctor asks.

And I will be fast.

"Actually," I reply, "I think I will just walk."

"Oh . . . okay," he says. He looks at the fat man, lifting his shoulders and his eyebrows. "Sure, we can do that."

The fat man leaves.

For three months I have been not allowed to walk on my leg because it has cancer so it could break if I put weight on it. But it does not matter anymore if it breaks because they are going to cut it off anyway. Like how garbage collectors are not careful with your trash bags when they throw them a long way into the garbage truck and they land with a loud crunch. There might be things in your trash bags that you saved up to buy and were very careful with for months but now they are getting thrown away so the garbage collectors don't have to worry about breaking them. So that is why I tell the doctors I will walk.

As I follow the doctor and the nurse down the hallway I feel the coldness of the floor under my brown socks. I know that coldness is the last thing I will ever feel in my left foot. I walk through a door into the operating room, which I know are the last steps I will ever take with two real legs. It's very bright. I sit myself down on the operating table. They put on the mask.

When I wake up from the operation, something is wrong. I can feel my leg propped straight up in the air. They . . . they . . . didn't cut it off! There's been a terrible mistake! I lift my head from the pillow to look down at it. Nothing . . . It's gone . . . It's definitely been amputated . . . but I still feel it in my mind just like I always have.

It is throbbing in pain. Not the kind of pain like I had from the cancer, though. No, this pain feels like my foot—the left foot that was just cut off—is being stabbed with thousands of tiny needles all at the same time. They are tearing down through my skin and stabbing the tendons and the muscles and now scraping into the bones.

Someone shows me the morphine button beside my bed, and I press it and feel warm. Doctors come and go. Machines beep. Bags of other people's blood drip into my port to replace all the blood I lost during the surgery.

About ten o'clock that night, a nurse with red hair tells me that she needs me to urinate, because I haven't emptied my bladder since the operation and she is afraid things haven't woken up yet down there. I am too weak to sit up, so Mom holds the jug for me as I lie flat on my back. But nothing comes out.

"Can't go, huh?" the nurse says.

"No."

"Okay, I'm going to have to put in a catheter."

"What's that?"

"It's a tiny tube that we will put in your—" She looks at Mom.

"Penis," Mom says.

"Yes, in your penis. It will drain your bladder for us."

A tube? A tube in my penis?

"Does it hurt?"

"Some people say it stings a little."

A little?

"How do you get it in?"

"We just push it in."

I shiver even though I am under so many blankets.

"How about—Can you please wait a few minutes?" I say. "I will go for you in the jug."

"I'm sorry. I have to."

"Wait, just wait a few more minutes. I will drink tons of water."

"Tell you what," she says. "Midnight. You have until midnight."

Mom fills up a cup of water at the sink, and I drink it down in a few sips. She fills it again, and I gulp that one, too. I drink cup after cup. And then we wait. I try to go in the jug at fifteen minutes after eleven. Nothing. At 11:30. Nothing. At 11:45. Still nothing. At 11:57, I try one last time.

Come on Joshua, come on! You have always been able to start and stop urinating when you need to! Remember? You can always . . . control . . . it . . . Yes! There it is! Done! No catheter for me, thank you very much Miss Nurse with Red Hair.

When the nurse with red hair comes back at midnight, I hold up the jug like a trophy.

"Look!"

She takes the jug and holds it in front of the light.

"Let me see here . . ."

What is there to see? I did it. You said by midnight, I did it by midnight. You promised!

"Sorry, that's not quite enough. I am going to have to give you a catheter."

Not quite enough? But before she only said by *midnight*. Not *a certain amount* by midnight, just that midnight was the deadline. She changed the rules, which everyone knows is cheating.

She rips open a large paper envelope and pulls out a long clear plastic tube. It looks way too thick to fit inside me. Is it the wrong tube? She takes a step toward me with the tube in her hand. I know pain is coming, very major pain. I start punching the morphine button beside my bed like it is the close-the-door button on an elevator and the bad guys chasing me are just down the hall. *Hurry! Close the doors! Pump the morphine!*

"This will only sting a little, I promise."

Yeah, right. I know how your promises work.

I expect the worst, but it is worse than the worst. It feels like she is stuffing barbed wire through a hole where it does not fit. Stuffing it . . . in . . . and it is shredding the insides of my insides. And just when I think it's over, the barbed wire turns red hot, and it burns, burns, burns the same gashes it is carving on the insides of my insides.

"There. That wasn't so bad, was it?"

Wasn't so bad?

"That was the worst pain I have ever felt," I say.

The nurse does not say anything, but she is probably thinking if what she did to me was the worst pain I've ever felt, that must be pretty bad considering I just had my leg cut off.

I wake up a few hours later and the tube hurts even more. I watch the second hand on the wall tick around in circles, minute by minute. This will get better. It has to. It can't get worse, right? I will feel better and finish chemotherapy, and my hair will grow back. I won't have to go into the hospital anymore and I won't have to have shots all the time and worry about dying. I will learn how to run with a fake leg and I will play sports and I will not wear a hospital gown, which looks like something you wear in a nursing home, a place where people die. But not me. I am going to live.

In the morning, a physical therapist comes to my room to teach me how to walk.

"Would it be all right if you come back tomorrow?" I say. "I have a—I just don't think I can move today."

This is true. I really can't move. There's the catheter, of course—that tube alone should be enough to stop us from talking about learning to walk right now. But I also have an IV pumping me with a who-knows-what mixture of postsurgery antibiotic things and painkillers, and another pump that has a dark red ziplock bag that is drip, drip, dripping blood into my veins to replace what I lost when my leg was cut off and all that blood that was supposed to flow into my leg started flowing out onto the operating table. And then there's *that* tube, that tube that is stuck inside me, in between the stitches that are holding my skin together across my pelvis where my leg used to be—that tube, it is the one the surgeon *left inside me* when he sewed me up. He wants it there for several days to collect drainage from the incision and sure enough there's a constant flow of thick yellowy pus and blood and pieces of flesh-colored clumps the size of crumbs oozing out.

"No, I think we should learn how to walk today. That's very important," the physical therapist says, as if her saying "we" will trick me into thinking we are on a team together. I know she is only trying to trick me because it is her job to help me get better and she thinks learning how to walk today will be good for me. But if she really wants to be on the same team together, she should listen to her teammate, who is me, and come back tomorrow like I said.

"I'm sorry. I just can't do it."

"Just try, okay? Please. All you have to do is try."

Her assistant is holding my crutches for me beside the bed. I sit up and the physical therapist puts her arms around me. It hurts.

"You're squeezing my port."

"Oh, sorry."

I put my foot on the carpet. I'm still wearing that same brown sock with the rubber strips on the bottom that I got when I checked in to the hospital. *What did they do with the sock on my left foot after the surgery?* When I try to stand, I fall straight into the physical therapist. I am much lighter than I used to be since all the leg weight is gone so the balance I remember in my mind doesn't work anymore. The assistant shoves the crutches under my arms.

"There you go. Try to take a step."

I do, and a pain shoots through my penis as the catheter rubs against the rawness inside.

"Aaaaah!" I say. "No more! I'm done! Let me back in bed!"

I ask Mom what happened to my leg after they cut it off. She says the doctors studied it for research. To research it, they opened it and looked inside. Like my leg was a book from the library.

The doctors found more cancer in my muscles around my bone, which means if we had tried to save my leg by putting in a metal bone or a dead person's bone, the doctors would have had to cut out a lot of muscles and my leg would have been very weak. So I decide that is another reason cutting off my leg was a very good idea. I ask what happened to my leg after they were done researching it, and Mom is not sure, maybe it was incinerated. I ask what that means and she says it means burned up in a hot fire. Which is a weird thing to have happen to a part of your body, but I guess it is the same thing that happens to the rest of your body after you die unless you are buried in a coffin. I wonder if I should have asked them to bury my leg in a coffin instead of incinerating it. But maybe it is better that it was burned up so I don't have to keep going to a cemetery to visit my leg which would be sad.

The next day, a doctor comes to examine me. He has short, dark hair combed back like mine used to be before it all fell out. He looks under my gown and tells me it is time to remove the drainage tube. I am very afraid of this. It hurts enough to pull a thin little *needle* out of your skin, and I know it will be worse if it is a *drainage tube* that's stuck between differently shaped sections of skin stitched together like pieces from two separate jigsaw puzzles. I ask the doctor to please, please, please leave it in for a few more days, or to give me anesthesia before he pulls it out, or to just come back later, maybe later today or tonight, and pull it out then. Just don't do it *now*.

"Joshua, it's not going to hurt. I promise."

I've heard that one before.

"Please! Just leave it!"

"How about I just look at it?"

"Okay, but don't pull it out."

"I won't even touch it."

"Promise?"

"Promise."

"All right."

He lifts up my gown and looks at the tube.

"Yeah, I think it's ready to come out," he says, smiling like he thinks this is good news.

"No! You promised!"

"Okay, I won't pull it out. Just let me touch it, and you can tell me if that hurts, all right?"

I look at Mom. She nods that this is a good plan.

"Okay. You promise you won't pull it out?"

He raises his right hand.

"Cross my heart, hope to die."

I wiggle my hand at Mom so she will know I want her to hold it and she does.

"Are you ready?"

"Yes."

I close my eyes and squeeze Mom's hand. The doctor touches the tube, but he does it so lightly I can barely feel it.

"Did that hurt?"

"No," I say. "It didn't."

He touches it again.

"How about that?"

"Nope," I say, my eyes still squeezed shut.

He touches it once more, a little bit harder, but it still doesn't hurt.

"Did that hurt?"

"No."

"Well, guess what."

"What?"

"It's out."

I open my eyes and see him standing there, holding the end of the pus-and-blood-and-other-stuff tube, smiling like he just pulled that tube out of thin air and we should clap for his magic trick.

"I told you it wouldn't hurt!"

"But . . . you raised your . . . You . . . you promised!"

I wish I wasn't still attached to so many other tubes and I knew how to balance on one leg, because if I could, I would hop out of bed and grab his white coat and push him against the wall. "You promised!" I would scream at him. "You broke your promise to me!"

"I'm sorry, Joshua. I just wanted to get it out for you," he says.

"You promised," I say. *And you kept a secret from me . . .*

He walks out carrying the tube in his hand and shaking his head.

My mind goes back to when I shared a room with Johnny. I think about when his mom hugged me but I didn't hug her back because she kept secrets from Johnny and didn't tell him he was dying. And I think about Mom and how she promised to never be like Johnny's mom. Then I feel Mom's hand, still in mine. I let go of her hand and turn my head to face her, but she looks away before we make eye contact. She looks down at the floor, and then she looks toward the ceiling.

When I am an adult, I am not going to make promises and break them or lie to kids. I am going to tell them the truth about everything, like telling them if they are going to die from cancer, and about how much catheters hurt, and about drainage tubes I am pulling out.

Two days later, while Mom is having a meeting with Dr. Dunsmore, I can tell that my catheter has something wrong with it. I need to urinate, but I feel like I am holding it inside the way I usually do when I don't have a catheter. I press the nurse button on the side of my bed. It beeps a few times. Then I hear a very loud voice coming out of the speaker right beside my head.

"Yes, Joshua?" the loud voice says.

"Hi, this is Joshua . . . Well, my catheter . . . I don't think it's working anymore."

"How do you know?"

"I can feel it. It doesn't feel right anymore. Can you please take it out?"

But the loud voice doesn't believe me.

"Why don't we just leave it in for now?"

"Well . . . I guess . . . it's just that I have to urinate and I don't think the catheter works anymore."

"Don't worry, Joshua. Just let it go. The catheter will get it."

Why don't you believe me?

"Okay, I will try," I say. "But I don't think it will work."

I hear a loud click from the speaker, and thirty seconds later my nursing-home-style hospital gown and the hospital sheets and even the crinkly plastic mattress are soaked in warm urine. It feels kind of nice like being in a hot tub except that I know it's not a hot tub and it's actually urine and that makes it feel disgusting.

"Uh-oh, did we have a little accident?" the nurse says when she comes to put a new bag on my IV.

But I don't say anything because *we* did not have an accident. *She* did. I told her it was not working anymore, and she did not believe me, so it's her accident.

"Well, don't you worry about it," she says. "This kind of thing happens all the time around here, Lord knows, especially when I used to work the night shift. So don't feel embarrassed."

I realize this must be a different nurse than the one on the speaker. This nurse thinks I am a bed wetter even though I am nine years old and I don't ever wet the bed anymore and it's really the nurse-on-the-speaker's fault.

"Well, I guess it's time for that catheter to come out, huh?"

It hurts almost as much coming out as it did going in.

Later that day, the physical therapist glues two stickers to my back, to the lower part of my back right above my underwear. There are wires coming out of these stickers, wires that will give me an electric shock—not the kind that electrocutes and kills people, no, don't worry, she says, this is a tiny shock I will barely feel. And this tiny electric shock will send a message to my brain that will block the pain from the thousands of tiny needles that are still stabbing my left foot, even now after the doctor gave me as much pain medicine as a nine-year-old can get at one time.

It is strange to have pain in a part of my body that is not there anymore. The doctors call this phantom limb pain because my leg is like a phantom, or a ghost, which makes sense because ghosts are not real and neither is my leg. But there is a part of my brain that has a map of my body, and the map thinks I still have a leg, like if a street was removed and covered with grass but still showing up on a road map. My brain keeps waiting to get nerve messages, feelings like hot or cold or socks or pants, from my leg. But since there are no messages coming in, my brain is confused, and the confusion makes my leg feel like there are thousands of tiny needles pricking my imaginary foot.

When the physical therapist turns the knob, the stickers with the wires coming out start burning holes through my skin, and my body is bouncing up and down and side to side on the bed. I try to stop bouncing, because you are not supposed to bounce on beds, especially hospital beds. But I can't stop. My body is bouncing automatically, the way my knee does when Dr. Marsh hits it with the orange triangle-shaped hammer. That's how I feel now, except my whole body feels like it has been hit with the hammer, and it's a big, heavy hammer like an orange triangle-shaped sledgehammer, so it's not just my knee but also my head, shoulders, elbows, belly button, and everything else in my body that is bouncing on the bed. And I can't hear anything, either, because it sounds like there are bees stuck in both of my ears that are buzzing so loudly they are shaking my brain.

Then the physical therapist presses a button and there is no more burning or bouncing or buzzing. She says that oh, she's so, so sorry and she accidentally started with level fifteen instead of level zero, which happened because she had the knob turned all the way to the right instead of the left, and now she will try again starting at zero and turn it up very, very slowly. But I tell her I don't want to get shocked by the stickers anymore because instead of stopping the needles from stabbing my foot, the stickers made me bounce up and down and put a buzzing noise in my head and almost burned holes through my skin, and all this hurts even more than the needles.

A few days after my amputation, Dr. Dunsmore says I am healing fast and I don't need any more blood or antibiotics pumped through my IV. So she pulls out the last tube, the one in my port.

They are all gone. I am free. Without the tubes rubbing all my insides and stopping me from moving, I decide to change into regular clothes. Mom helps me pull the hospital gown off my shoulders and down my arms and then I lean back in the bed so I can pull on a pair of shorts. I hold the shorts out to the side so my left leg can go into them because that's what I do automatically without thinking about how I don't have that leg anymore. I feel that left leg pass through the shorts and then float *inside* the mattress, like a ghost.

I don't like having my leg inside the mattress like a ghost because that is impossible. So I think about the leg—the imaginary leg—very carefully in my mind, and after a few seconds I am able to straighten the ghost knee so it's not inside the mattress anymore. Now I can feel it sitting on top of the bed like my real leg. Which is much better.

I put on a T-shirt and stand up and lean against the bed. The other day when the physical therapist made me stand up, there were so many tubes in my body. I was chained by the IV in the port in my chest, the catheter, the heart monitor on my finger, the drainage tube in the place where my leg used to be—but now I stand and I feel free and light. No more chains. And no more cancer hanging off my body.

Mom hands me my crutches, and I slide them under my shoulders. I put the crutches on the floor in front of my foot and then I lean onto them and swing forward. All my weight seems to be pushing on my left crutch. I feel like I am falling to the left. So I have to tilt my body to the right so I don't fall.

This is called a new center of gravity which I know because I read a brochure of ten tips for people who are thinking about losing their legs. Mom has given me lots of brochures and also some books about people without legs. The first thing we did once I knew my leg might get cut off was Mom took me to the public library. Mom said this is the best and cheapest way to solve the problems in your life: come to the library and check out all the books about your problem and read them.

When I used to stand with two legs I would put weight on both of them so my belly button was halfway in between my feet. Now when I stand I can only put weight on one leg so to balance my belly button has to be above my one foot. I keep practicing finding my new center of gravity all morning, and by the afternoon I am running laps around my floor of the hospital by hopping on my foot in between each step on my crutches. I am fast because I don't have a heavy leg filled with cancer. The physical therapist chases after me in her squeaky tennis shoes, saying I need to take it easy.

On the fifth day after my amputation, Dr. Dunsmore comes in and tells me I can go home.

"But it hasn't been three weeks yet," I say.

The plan had always been that I would be here for three weeks after the amputation. I brought tons of books and games and drawing pads because three weeks is a very long time to be in the hospital. Matthew and Luke were going to come visit me next week. No one knew I was going to get released so early. Except God since he knows everything.

"Well, you healed much faster than we anticipated. And your vital signs have stabilized," she says. She tells me they'd like me to go home and rest for a few weeks before my next chemo treatment.

A few hours before I leave to go home Dr. Dunsmore sends a psychologist to examine me for the depression, which is a sadness the brochures said people feel after amputations. But I do not feel sad anymore. I used to feel sad, before the surgery. While I was waiting for the day of the surgery to come, every night I would lie in the bottom bunk and cry until I fell asleep. But now I feel happy because the surgery is over which means the cancer that was in my leg is gone and all the tubes are pulled out from my body. I heard Dr. Dunsmore telling Mom in the hallway that even if I show no outward symptoms of depression I might be repressing my feelings. Mom said a lot of people have been praying for me and maybe I'm just a very happy little boy.

The psychologist comes to my hospital room while I am drawing, and she says she would like to draw with me for a few minutes.

"Would you please tell me about what you are drawing?" she asks.

This is a silly question because she should know what I am drawing. It's a picture of Zorro, the secret identity of Don Diego de la Vega. He has a cape and an eye mask and a big, round hat.

"Don't you know who it is?" I ask.

"Yes, of course I know who that is," she says, smiling. "But I want you to tell me about it. Can you tell me why you decided to draw that picture? Or how it makes you feel?"

I don't like how she could not recognize my picture of Zorro because I have taken art lessons for three years and I am good at drawing. So I stop answering her questions.

She gets out a piece of paper and starts coloring a picture of her own. While she is bent over her page, I look at the top of her head and see that she has wavy brown hair that is clumped together the way mine used to be before it fell out, when I used to put lots of gel in it every day. Then I look at her drawing. It's pretty good, but I don't say anything nice to her about it since she was not nice when she did not know what I was drawing. Eventually she says goodbye and leaves.

A few days later, after I'm home, Mom and Dad get a bill from the psychologist for four hundred dollars. Insurance will pay for it, but four hundred dollars is still a lot of money. It's enough to buy almost anything, really, even expensive things like bikes or Nintendos. I can't believe we have to pay that much to a psychologist who said not-nice things when she talked about my Zorro picture.

"That psychologist missed her calling in life," Mom says. "If she can charge that much for fifteen minutes of drawing, she should have become an artist."

Mom usually doesn't tell funny jokes, but this is very funny.

6

It's the end of July, just a couple weeks after my surgery. That's usually when we go to Lost River State Park for the church-wide vacation. Matthew was really looking forward to going this year, since last year he was only six and wasn't old enough to play with the big kids and adults in the annual softball game. He wanted to play this year to try to hit a home run even though that's pretty much impossible in softball especially for a seven-year-old. But it doesn't matter anyway because we can't go this year since I have to get my shots.

When I am not in the hospital I have to have a shot every day. A couple months ago I used to be very afraid of needles and I cried whenever people wanted to stab me with them. But now I am more used to them. I always put an ice pack from the freezer on the part of my skin that is going to get stabbed to make it numb. I am not sure it helps, because the shots still hurt. But I don't cry anymore. Now I just close my eyes and hold Mom's hand.

I have the shots every day when I am at home so my body will get ready for more chemotherapy. Chemo is not a smart medicine. It does not know how to tell the difference between cancer cells and good cells. The only thing it can tell is if it is a *fast-growing* cell. That helps it find cancer because cancer is just cells that are broken in a way that makes them grow way too fast.

When chemo finds any fast-growing cells, it tries to kill them. Which is good if the cell is cancer. But there are also good cells that are fast growing, like hair cells. That is why chemo made my hair fall out. Another fast-growing cell is immune system cells, which try to help my body not get sick. So chemo hurts my immune system, and too much of it would make my immune system so weak that I could get really sick and die from a cold or if I scraped my knee and it got infected. The shots I have every day are to help my immune system grow new cells so I can get more chemo without dying.

Four months ago, when I was first starting the chemo, a nurse came to our house every day to give me the shot. But then our insurance company said they would not pay for the nurse anymore because it was too expensive, so I had two choices: I could either give myself a shot every day, or Mom could do it.

The first option would never work. I would be too afraid and I would just sit there and look at the needle for an hour or two, and then I would probably throw it away and lie and tell Dr. Dunsmore I had given myself the shot even though I hadn't and even though lying is wrong. So Mom said okay, she would be willing to give me a shot every day all year since I didn't think I could do it myself.

The night after Mom said she would give me the shots I had a dream where Mom chased me with needles and threw them at me like I was a dartboard. I woke up sweating and breathing fast, and walked on my crutches down the hall and got in bed with Mom and Dad. When I told Mom about the dream, Mom started crying even though it was just a dream and dreams aren't real.

But the next day a nurse from our church called Mom and said that she would come over every day after work for the whole year to give me a shot for free. Mom said the nurse was an answer to prayer, which is what you say when something happens that you hoped would happen so you whispered it to God before bed. Not all people think God is real, but I am glad I know he is because it makes cancer less scary. I know God has a plan for me even if I do not understand or like the plan. Someday when I get to heaven, I will see the plan and it will make sense why I had cancer and my leg got cut off even if it does not make sense now.

Before my operation the nurse who was an answer to prayer gave me a shot in my right arm one day, left arm the next day, right leg after that, and then left leg. So it used to be a four-day cycle. Now it's three days.

I tell Mom and Dad how much I want to go to Lost River because all my friends from church will be there. They ask Dr. Montgomery if he can give me the shots since he's a doctor and he says yes so Mom and Dad decide I can go to Lost River for two nights! Yes . . . *two nights!* It will be so fun. I will stay with the Montgomerys, who are allowed to watch TV and eat as much candy as they want. This will be great because Matthew and I are only allowed to eat one piece of candy per week, on Candy Day, which is Friday. I wish the Montgomerys had invited Matthew, too.

● ● ●

It is scary when I walk into the Montgomerys' cabin for the first time. I have to walk slowly on my crutches up the step through the front door because my balance is not very good. And then they all see me. It is the first time anyone besides my family and people at the hospital have seen me since my leg got cut off. I look very different than I did before because one side of my shorts is hanging empty like an American flag when there is no wind. Everyone tries to look at my eyes instead of my missing leg but I can understand how they want to look down because when I look in the mirror I also look there since it is very surprising to see one leg instead of two.

I want everyone to find out I am still the same person on the inside even though I look really different on the outside. That is why I am happy to be at Lost River, where I can show everyone I can still do things I did before like play games and sports and talk and laugh at jokes. So it's great the Montgomerys let their kids and me stay up really late in the upstairs loft of their cabin, talking and laughing. The next morning, after I eat sweet cereal for breakfast, Dr. Montgomery asks me to come to his bedroom so he can give me my shot. So I walk into the bedroom on my crutches and one leg and Mrs. Montgomery sits with me on the bed and holds my hand just like Mom does when I get shots at home. And I don't cry because even though it hurts I get shots every day so I know how they feel.

That afternoon, Dr. Montgomery asks me if there is anything I want to talk about. I say like what. He says that Karen (he gets to call his wife by her first name since he is a grown-up) told him maybe there was stuff I would want to talk about. I say no. It's a strange question to ask me because if there was something I needed to talk to him about, I would have already talked about it. But before I had cancer and my leg got cut off, grown-ups never asked me if there was anything I wanted to talk about. So I guess he is probably asking if I want to talk about that. But talking will not make the cancer go away or bring my leg back from the incinerator. So I do not want to talk. I want to go outside and play.

We all go to the annual softball game, and I am sorry Matthew won't be here to play in it since he was looking forward to it all year. So I decide I will play for him and I will tell him about it when I get home.

There are two captains who will pick the teams for the game. I'm sure no one will pick me because I have one leg and they will think I am not good at softball. Or they might not pick me because they do not know I want to play since they have probably never seen a boy with no hair and no left leg play in a softball game. So I walk over to the captains. One of them is Pastor Smuland, and the other is Tim, who I know because he is also homeschooled and comes to homeschool potlucks. Tim is pretty old, probably sixteen or seventeen. He is very good at shooting rubber bands and even has a slingshot for firing rocks at squirrels. Before I got cancer, I used to play homeschool soccer with him. Tim is the best soccer player I've ever seen. I used to want to be just like Tim, but now I cannot ever be like him since he has two legs and I don't.

"I'm going to play in the softball game," I tell Tim and Pastor Smuland.

They look confused, probably because they think I can't run. So I take off on my crutches for about twenty feet and then run back.

"Wow, *awesome!*" Pastor Smuland says, slapping me a high five. Mom always says people want to be Pastor Smuland's friend because he is very enthusiastic and now I understand what she means. "Aaaaaaall right! That's what I'm *talkin'* about, baby! Ha! Can you hit the ball, too?"

I have not really thought about this. *Hmmmmm.* For me to swing, I would have to put my crutches down so I could hold the bat. But then after I hit the ball I would have to bend over and pick up my crutches before I could start running. This would take so long I would probably get tagged out so I maybe I can't play after all—

"I will run for him," Tim says. "Joshua can hit the ball, and then I'll run to first base."

"Yeah—yeah, okay," Pastor Smuland says.

Tim keeps talking.

" . . . And when the next batter gets to the plate, Joshua and I will switch bases and he can run the rest of the way."

I nod. This is a great plan.

And it will be Tim running for me—*Tim!* I sometimes used to pretend I was Tim when I was playing sports. But today when he runs in my place Tim will be pretending he is me.

"Okay, let's do it!" Pastor Smuland says.

When they are picking teams, Tim points at me.

"Joshua," he says.

He picks me *second*, so he must have been really impressed by how fast I can run on my crutches. But while I am walking over to Tim—leaving all those unlucky people who didn't get picked second—I see Dad's car drive into the parking lot beside the softball field.

Oh, no, please . . . not *now* . . . I don't want to go home yet! Not right before the annual softball game! It's only been one night and I was supposed to get to stay for two!

Dad parks and walks over to me while Tim and Pastor Smuland keep picking teams.

"What are you doing here?" I ask Dad, trying to make my voice sound sad so he will know I don't want to leave yet.

"Hi, Joshua," he says, hugging me. "I just came to visit you."

"Wait . . . visit—so I don't have to go home now?"

"No, you can stay until tomorrow."

"Yessssss!" I say, pumping my fist.

Dad laughs.

"What's so funny?" I ask.

"Oh, nothing," he says.

But I know something was funny. That is why he laughed.

"Okay I have to go play softball now," I say.

"You're playing softball?"

I am afraid Dad will say I am not allowed to.

"Yeah I'm on Tim's team. He's going to run for me."

I tell him this so he knows I am already on a team, which means he can't tell me to drop out because then the teams would be uneven.

"Oh . . . okay," Dad says. "Well . . . I guess . . . I will be rooting for you!"

When it's my turn to go to bat, I walk over and lay my crutches on the ground about five feet behind the catcher. Then I hop to home plate and pick up the bat. At first I try to stand upright and put the bat on my shoulder, but I keep losing my balance and having to put the bat down to stay standing, like the bat is a cane. It's embarrassing to not have good enough balance to stand without leaning on the bat. I'm like Luke when he was a baby who did not know how to walk yet. But at least I don't fall in front of Tim and Dad and all my friends. *Just don't fall.* It is very important never to fall, especially when other people are watching. If they see you fall, all your friends will think you can't do stuff like play sports anymore.

I look at Tim, and he is bent over with the tips of his fingers in the dirt, like a sprinter at the start of a race. He is waiting for me to get a hit.

"Ready?" asks Pastor Smuland from his place on the pitcher's mound.

I nod.

He throws the ball underhand, a big, slow throw that arcs through the air. Right as the ball is coming across the plate, I pick up the bat, draw it back over my shoulder, and then swing as hard as I can.

Whooosh.

I miss and the force of the swing spins my body around and I lose my balance and the bat goes flying toward the fence behind the catcher. I land in a cloud of dry baseball dust. I take a breath and start coughing.

Pastor Smuland comes running from the pitcher's mound.

"Joshua! You all right?"

"Yes," I say. "I'm fine. Kind of dusty, though."

I try to laugh a little because everyone knows that if you are laughing, you must be all right. People who stop laughing are always the ones who get hurt.

I stand up and brush the dust off my pants and then clap to get it off my hands, too.

"Here you go."

Tim hands me the bat.

"Thanks."

Pastor Smuland throws me another pitch, another high, slow one just like the first, and I swing and miss and fall down again in the dust. I get back up, and now it's my third pitch. I have to hit this one, or else I will be struck out and Tim will be sorry he picked me for his team because I am not good.

"Come on, Joshua!"

It's Dad. I turn and see him standing behind the chain-link fence, halfway between home plate and first base. His fingers are poked through, gripping tight to the fence wire.

"You can do it!" he says.

There are tons of people from church here all watching the game, but I can easily hear Dad because the other people are not making any noise. They are all just standing along the fence not talking. I look at them to find out why they are so quiet and I see that they are all looking at me.

When we used to play baseball in the backyard, Dad always said keep your eye on the ball. So that's what I do on the third pitch. I watch carefully as it flies very, very slowly through the air spinning forward and falling lower and lower as it comes toward me. I can see Pastor Smuland behind the ball still standing on his front leg with his arm reaching forward. *But wait no don't look at Pastor Smuland! Keep your eye on the—where is it?—there! Swing! Now! Whoosh.* I swing and miss. I fall in the dust. I am out. Tim is sorry he picked me and Dad feels sad about being my dad and cheering for me.

I get up and hop over to my crutches.

"Hold on, Joshua," Pastor Smuland says. "Keep going."

"But I'm out," I say.

"You're not out yet," he says.

I am confused since I got three strikes, so I should be out. But Pastor Smuland is in charge so if he says I am not out then I will keep swinging. I will get a hit! Everyone will cheer!

But Pastor Smuland gives me four more pitches, and I miss and fall in the dust every time. Suddenly I am breathing the way you do right before you start crying. I will let my friends see me fall in the dust but I will not let them see me cry. So I drop the bat and hop over to my crutches and pick them up to run away from the field. But after I take a few steps I hear Dad.

"Joshua," Dad says, "you almost *had* that last one!"

I look at him over there holding the chain-link fence.

"It was *this close*," he says, sticking two fingers through the fence and making a space of about two inches.

There are so many people here, people who shaved their heads for me, who made shirts at Vacation Bible School with my name on them and who come to my house and play computer games with me when I can't go outside to play. I can't let them see me cry, but I can't let them see me strike out either. So I hop back to the plate and pick up the bat and nod at Pastor Smuland.

"Batter up," Tim says, giving me a thumbs-up and bending down like a track runner again.

I miss the next pitch, but this time I don't let go of the bat and don't fall down. After I swing, I put the bat down on the ground like a cane to steady my balance. I hear some people behind me whispering. I keep getting strikes, but I also keep not falling. More strikes. Strike, strike, strike. So many strikes I lose count. Then one time I swing and I hear a *twink* and feel the contact between the bat and ball in my hands. The ball rolls forward on the ground, straight toward the shortstop. The ball is rolling very slowly so I know the shortstop will run toward it and pick it up and throw it to first before Tim can run there. But instead, the shortstop bends over and puts his open glove on the ground and just waits for the ball.

By the time the ball gets to him Tim is already safe at first base. Even with all of them cheering and clapping, I can easily hear Dad when he says, "Way to go, Joshua." After the play is over Tim switches with me. I come onto first base because I can run with my crutches. My team gets a series of base hits. I go to second. Then third. Then I cross home plate and score a point for my team. Everyone cheers. Even people on the other team clap and tell me great job, which is weird since they are losing because of me. It feels very good even though I fell a bunch of times which I guess means falling is okay if you keep getting back up until you get a hit.

7

It's time for me to be fitted with a fake leg, which is called a prosthesis. I can't wait. I have seen photos of amputees wearing fake legs and playing soccer. I also have a poster on my wall of two amputees who are wearing tight USA tank tops and running on a track with their fake legs on. I would like to be on a poster like that.

The doctor at Johns Hopkins told me I won't ever be able to run with a fake leg because my amputation is too high. He said most amputees have their legs cut off farther down, so they still have hip muscles to use for running. But I know that he is wrong because my whole life anytime I have ever heard people tell stories like "Doctors said I would never walk again" or "Doctors said I would never come out of the coma," the next thing the people always say is how they did exactly the thing the doctors told them they would never be able to do. They walked again. They came out of the coma. So you should not listen to the doctors when they tell you never again.

Getting fitted for a fake leg is very messy. There is a man called a prosthetist who wraps your body from below your arms all the way down to your knee (the one that wasn't cut off) with strips of fabric that drip white liquid all over the floor. The strips dry and get very hard and you can't move. This will be the mold for the socket, he says, which is the part of the leg that attaches to your body. Then the prosthetist gets out something that looks like a small chainsaw and he cuts the cast so he can take it off your body and talks about how he will try not to slip with the saw because you already lost one of your legs, ha ha.

Then the prosthetist has you stand up against a piece of paper on the wall and he holds a pencil against your skin and traces your whole leg like at Thanksgiving when you trace your hand on paper to make a drawing of a turkey. Then you hop away from the wall and look at the drawing and you can see how your thigh is much wider than your knee because there are so many muscles in it.

You have to decide what color skin you want. The prosthetist has a book with a piece of rubber skin glued to each page and you flip through it and choose the color you want. It's like the book with little pieces of carpet at the hardware store that you look at when your family is trying to decide what kind of carpet to get in the living room. You ask the prosthetist why there are twelve different kinds of skin for white people and only three for Black people. He says "um" a few times and then says it is because that's the way the skin company makes the skin which doesn't really answer your question.

My fake leg, when it is finished, is very uncomfortable. This is surprising since the leg costs as much as a fancy car and fancy cars are very, very comfortable. The leg wraps around the middle of my body like a one-inch-thick diaper made out of hard plastic. The place where my leg was removed—the prosthetist calls it a "stump," but Mom calls it a "residual limb" because she thinks this sounds better—is very sore so it hurts to have the hard plastic pressing against it.

The leg is very heavy. The prosthetist says it actually only weighs ten pounds, which he says is half as much as my real leg weighed before it got cut off. But when I still had my real leg, I didn't ever think, *Wow, this leg is really heavy. I would like to take it off.* But that's what I think about all the time when I wear my fake one.

I have to learn how to walk again, too. The physical therapist who will teach me is named Bev. She is very old and you can tell she has grandchildren because she is very nice. On the first day, she gets out a big book, as big as a dictionary, and sets it down on the table.

"Let's see here," she says, turning the pages in the book. "Hip. *H-H-H-I-I* . . . Okay, here we are: 'hip disarticulation.'" She scans the page. "It says here that you should be able to learn how to walk just fine," she says. "What else? Carrying. Okay, you won't be able to carry anything, especially books, so that might make it hard at school."

"I am homeschooled."

"What?"

"My mom teaches me. I go to school at home."

"So you don't have books?"

"No, I have books, but I don't have to carry them anywhere because they're already on my desk."

"Oh, okay, good," she says. "What about stairs? Do you have any stairs?"

"Yes."

"How many flights?"

"Five or six."

She looks very surprised.

"Five or six flights?" Bev asks.

"No, no," Mom says. "*Stairs.* Five or six stairs, leading up to the front porch. Our house is all on one level; it's a ranch. No flights."

"Perfect!" Bev says with a smile.

"And actually my husband just put a railing on those stairs," Mom says. "To help Joshua."

Whenever Mom is talking about Dad with people who don't know him, she calls him "my husband." But when Dad is talking about Mom with people who don't know *her*, he says "my wife, Linda," like he needs to tell the person which of his wives he is talking about even though he is only married to Mom.

"A railing, that's great," Bev says.

"What about running?" I ask, thinking about my poster of the amputees running on their fake legs.

"What about running?" Bev repeats my question.

"Yes."

"Well, let's see . . ."

She looks at the page.

"Nope."

"What do you mean?"

"You can't run."

"Not at all?"

"Well . . . there's something you can do that is sort of like running. I can teach you on your last day—how many days do you have scheduled right now?"

"Four," Mom says.

"Right, four," Bev says. "So, after your four days, I want you to go home for two weeks and get used to your prosthesis. Then come back and I will teach you how to run the best way you can. Here, I will show you. It will look kind of like this—"

She stands up, this grandmother physical therapist, and does a very weird thing. It's like she is skipping, but only with one of her legs. The other leg is walking. So she takes a normal step on one foot and then skips a step on the other. Step, skip, step, skip.

"That's the best you will be able to do because your prosthesis won't swing through fast enough to do a normal run," she says.

Of course, I know she is wrong about this. Probably she just has to run like that because she is a grandmother.

At the end of the four days of physical therapy, I can walk on my fake leg without a cane or crutches or handrails. I can even walk carrying that big book in my hands, the book that says I won't be able to carry books.

Then I go back to the hospital for another round of chemotherapy. I wear my fake leg and it looks pretty real since the prosthetist traced my leg and I chose a really good skin color. The only part that doesn't look real is the knee, which gets wrinkled when it bends. That's why I will only wear really long shorts from now on.

Before my leg got cut off, Mom always made me wear shorts that stopped above my knees. She said long shorts were for hooligans. But now that I have a fake leg that has a wrinkly knee, she cut off some of my old jeans into long shorts that cover up the knee and its wrinkles so you can't tell it's fake. And Mom and Dad let me wear one of these pairs of shorts to church on Sunday! A lot of people at church came over to look at the new leg and talk about how they couldn't tell which one was fake. People at the hospital like the leg, too. All the nurses come over and nod with their hands on their hips about my skin color being the right choice. Perfect match, they all say.

When you are in the hospital, there are people who come to your room every day. They are called residents because they live at the hospital. They ask you lots of questions about what you ate and how much you've urinated and also they take your temperature and blood pressure and pulse.

On the second day of this trip to the hospital, one of the residents is doing his exam and he looks at his watch, and then, still looking at the watch, he puts two fingers on my artificial leg. I know he is trying to get a pulse, but he won't get it there because there is no blood in my fake leg. So he will think I am dead. And then he will think it is very strange that I have been talking to him about what I ate and how much I've urinated even though I'm dead. Maybe he will think I am a ghost even though ghosts aren't real.

"Did you know that Joshua has a prosthesis?" Mom asks.

"What?" the resident says.

"Joshua has a prosthesis. It looks like you are trying to take a pulse from it," Mom says.

"Oh—what? Prosthesis. Oh—right, of course. Yes, it says it right here," he says, looking at his clipboard. "Yes, right—uh—well, I just remembered I have a meeting I am late for."

Then he walks out of the room very quickly because he is running late for his meeting.

After I finish the five days of chemo treatments, Mom takes me back to Bev the grandmother physical therapist to learn how to run. Bev shows me that same walk-skip-walk-skip thing she did before.

"Now you try," she says. "Just skip a step on your right foot while you wait for the prosthetic foot to swing through."

I try it. When I had two legs, if I wanted to run, I would just straighten my leg really fast and put it on the ground in front of my body. But with my fake leg, there are no muscles to make the knee straighten out fast. Instead, it hangs from my body and swings underneath me, powered by springs. With each step I have to wait for it to swing and then for the heel to hit the ground in front of me. It swings soooooo slooooooowly, like the long piece of metal that swings back and forth inside Nana and

Papa's big grandfather clock, the one that chimes every fifteen minutes even when you want to fall asleep.

I try very hard and I even pray and ask God to make my fake leg swing faster but God doesn't help and it still swings slowly and the only kind of running I can do is the step, skip, step, skip. Just like Bev showed me on my first day. It's not really running. More like half skipping. On the drive home from physical therapy, Mom asks why I am so quiet.

"Aren't you excited? You learned how to run today!" she says.

"Yeah . . . of course," I say, even though I am not excited.

But maybe Mom can tell from my voice that I am not actually excited because she doesn't ask me any more questions for the whole hour-long drive home. Maybe she is thinking what I am thinking: In the history of the world, I am the first person the doctors have ever been right about. They told me that I would never run again, and it's true. I won't.

8

Whenever I'm home people come visit me. Usually people from church, but sometimes they are people I don't even know. We sit in the family room with the visitors and they ask me questions about my cancer. But they never ask any questions to Matthew so he usually gets bored and leaves the room which makes me feel sad. They also don't ask Luke questions, but that makes sense because he doesn't speak English yet. Sometimes visitors even bring me presents. I asked Mom once why people give me so many presents and she said because I have cancer and I asked why that meant I should get presents though and she said people want to show they care. But they never bring presents for Matthew, so I always give him the ones I don't want after they leave.

I am usually home for two weeks, and then I go back to the hospital for almost a week, and then I come home for two weeks again. Unless I get an infection or fever and have to go back to the hospital an extra time. When I am in the hospital, which is an hour away from our house, Grandma takes a bus for twelve hours from Florida or Nana and Papa drive in their camper for four hours to our house to take care of Matthew and Luke. On weekdays Mom stays with me in the hospital because Dad has to go to work. On Friday after he finishes work Dad comes to stay with me and Mom drives home. Whoever is staying with me sleeps beside my hospital bed in a chair that can turn into a bed. The only time I am by myself is on Sunday morning when Dad goes to a church near the hospital. After church, he brings me back a Junior Bacon Cheeseburger from Wendy's as a reward for being in the hospital by myself. It is hard when Dad is at church because he is gone for two hours and usually I urinate into the jug every hour. While he is at church I just hold the urine inside because I do not want to hold the jug myself or have a nurse hold it and watch me urinate. One Sunday I can't hold it in and when Dad comes back with my Junior Bacon Cheeseburger there is urine all over me and my bed.

We get visited at our house by a TV crew. They are making a video for a show called *Children's Miracle Network Hospitals*, which will raise money to help buy medicine for families who have a sick child and not much money, like Johnny's parents. A cameraperson, a sound person, and a director come to our house to film me. The director is from Los Angeles and he wears three-hundred-dollar sunglasses. I know they cost that much because Matthew thought they were really cool and wanted to buy a pair and asked how much they cost. But Matthew doesn't have three hundred dollars because he's only seven.

Before the interview the director and I sit in my bedroom and talk about chemotherapy. I tell him how I go into the hospital one week out of every three weeks and lie in bed at the hospital because I am too tired to do anything. I tell him how when I am home I lie in bed, too, and how a nurse from church comes to give me a shot every day after she gets off work. I tell him how I am never hungry because chemotherapy makes food taste like metal and how I lost so much weight that last summer I only weighed sixty-eight pounds before my amputation and got as low as fifty-three pounds after. And I tell him how Mom now makes me eat lots of food so I will stop losing weight, even food that I am usually not allowed to eat because it gives you heart attacks like whole milk.

"And how old are you?" he asks.

"I just turned ten."

"That's a lot for a ten-year-old to deal with."

"I guess."

"What keeps you going?"

"Well . . . my family . . . because they really love me," I say. "Also, different people from our church make dinner for us every night, and they take care of Matthew and Luke whenever I am in the hospital. And some people from church come and clean our house, too, all for free."

"Yeah, well, that's really great," the director says. "But what keeps *you* going? What gets you out of bed in the morning?"

When he asks his question that way I know the answer. Every morning when I wake up, before I move the sheets off my body, I think about one thing.

"I want to finish."

I want to get done with chemotherapy, get done with hospitals, get done with shots. I want to see my hair grow back and I want food to taste good again, and I want to have energy. I want to not have cancer. I know now that I will never run. I will never play soccer. But at least one day I can wake up and have a normal life like I did before.

After we talk about all this the director interviews me in front of a camera and two lights that are so bright and hot they make me sweat. Then he interviews Mom and Dad. Dad cries while he says his answer to every question except the first one when they ask him how to spell his name. He even cries when the director asks him, "How will you feel when Joshua is done with chemotherapy?" which is actually something you should be happy about.

After the interview, when they are turning off the lights, Matthew walks in.

"Hey do you want to interview me, too?" Matthew asks.

"Well, no, I don't think we have time for that today," the director says.

Matthew frowns and his shoulders fall down.

"Hey, kid," the director says, patting Matthew on the back. "Just be glad that you're not the one who might die from cancer, right?"

Matthew nods.

We watch the director and his assistants pack up the lights and cameras and electrical cords into black bags and black boxes. Then they carry it all to the van outside. Dad helps them carry the bags and boxes, but no one asks me to help. That's one thing

I've noticed about having one leg: people don't ask you to help them push wheelbarrows of mulch or trim bushes in the back-yard anymore. You wish they would, though, because you want them to know you are strong and soon you'll be as strong as Dad. But no one ever asks.

Mom and Dad and I stand on the porch and wave goodbye to the director and his assistants as they drive away in their van. They wave back at us.

We walk back inside, and I go into my bedroom. Matthew is standing on the edge of my mattress on the bottom bunk. The cloth belt from his bathrobe is tied around the railing of the top bunk, and the other end is tied in a knot that he is tightening around his neck.

"Awwww*wwwww*!" I say. "You're in trouble! I'm gonna tell Mom!"

In our family we are never, ever allowed to tie anything around our necks or point guns at other people—even if it is a toy gun, because you never know when it might be a real gun and it might be loaded—and both of these rules, the no-putting-things-around-your-neck rule and the no-pointing-guns rule, are the most important rules in our house, so if you break them you get in very big trouble.

"Mommm!" I yell, stepping back into the hallway. "Matthew is putting a rope around his neck!"

Mom has bad hips from playing softball in high school. So she doesn't like steps or running. That's why she and Dad chose a one-story house with only five stairs to the front porch. But when I call her to tell her that Matthew has broken one of the most important rules, she comes running down the hallway and almost knocks me over when she turns the corner into our bedroom.

"Oh, Matthew!" she says. "Oh—*oh*. Paul! *Paul!*"

But Dad is already here, too, because he heard me yell about Matthew breaking the rule. I have never seen Dad's face look the way it does when he sees Matthew standing on the edge of the bed with the fabric belt tied around his neck. I can tell he has the same feelings I had when I thought the dogs were going to kill Matthew and me at Nana and Papa's house. Dad makes a noise. It's a noise like he is in pain, like he just stepped barefoot on a sharp rock in the backyard.

"Yaaa—*aaaaah!*"

Dad scoops up Matthew from the bottom bunk and holds him like a baby.

"Get it off! Get it off, Linda!" Dad says.

"I'm trying!" Mom says.

Mom is trying to untie the knot around Matthew's neck, but her hands are shaking so she can't grab hold of it. Finally she gets one of her fingers inside the knot and loosens it so she can slide it off Matthew and Dad bends his knees very fast and falls beside the bunk bed and holds Matthew's head against his shoulder. Mom is trying to hold Matthew, too, and she falls against Dad and they all tip back until they are lying on the floor.

Mom and Dad and Matthew are all crying, and now Luke walks in and starts crying, too. I am the only one who is not crying and I don't understand why Matthew isn't getting in big trouble. He broke the *most important rule*, and he almost hanged himself, which means he could have *died*. But I can tell from how Mom and Dad are crying that I shouldn't ask why he's not getting in trouble for any of this.

I sit on the edge of my bed and pull the end of my shorts up so I can feel the wrinkles in the rubber skin around my fake knee. I rub the wrinkles for a long time while everyone lies on the floor and cries, and Luke walks in and out of the room, still crying, too.

"Matthew, we love you so much," Mom says. "You are *so special* to us."

"Matthew . . ." Dad starts to speak, but then he starts crying again and can't talk.

Mom strokes Matthew's hair, which is still very short since he still shaves it to help me not feel bad.

"Sweetheart," she says, "can you tell us why you did that?"

Matthew looks at her, and then he looks over at me.

"Because," Matthew says, "if Joshua is going to die, I don't want to live anymore."

Going to die? He thinks I am going to *die*? He thinks the cancer will kill me? No way! Not a chance! I am going to *finish*!

I slide off the bed and grab Matthew's hand.

"Don't worry," I say. "I am not going to die."

"You're not?" he asks.

"No, I'm not."

"Promise?"

"Yeah, I promise."

• • •

Mom and I go to the hospital for chemo, but a nurse draws blood and comes back later saying my immune system has not grown back enough.

"Your blood counts are just too low, Joshua," she says. "Wait a week. Then come see us again."

Dr. Dunsmore warned us a long time ago that this might happen.

When you first start chemo, your immune system can grow back in just a few days after it is killed by the chemotherapy. But after nine months, it can start getting tired. Then you have to wait longer between treatments. Dr. Dunsmore said some kids' immune systems get so tired they end up being on chemotherapy for an extra year.

This makes me feel scared. Nine months ago when food started tasting like metal and my eyebrows fell out and I was too tired to play with Matthew in the backyard, I didn't think I could make it through a whole year of chemo. It was too hard and too long—one year is a tenth of my whole life, since I am ten now. But I decided I could get through one year of chemotherapy if every day I thought about finishing. Thinking about that made me feel strong. *Finishing*. That's what made me decide I could make it through the year, and that's why I told the director of the TV show with the three-hundred-dollar sunglasses that finishing is what keeps me going. So I promised myself I could make it through one year. But no more.

Since I can't get chemo today, we will have to drive an hour back home to Harrisonburg. It will be a very sad drive because I've always thought I would be finished after one year. That's all I think about.

When I'm finished I will start using LA Looks Gel, Level Five Most Extreme Hold, again! I will play outside! I will have eyebrows! I will get the top bunk bed back from Matthew! . . . Or, actually, maybe I will let him keep it, since he has been very sad recently and now he has to go to Purcell Park with a man from church who is trying to help him feel happy. But even if I stay on the bottom at least I will never ever have to sleep in a hospital bed again after I finish chemo.

I will still have to *go inside* the hospital every three months to get X-rays and CAT scans but these will never be overnight visits. And even if someday I have scans and Dr. Dunsmore looks at them and says the cancer has come back, I still won't have to spend the night in the hospital because I will tell her I don't want to start chemotherapy again because I will be finished.

Dr. Kimberly Dunsmore, my main doctor, always carries a clipboard, and when she writes on it she leans her head to one side so her hair falls in that direction. One time Dr. Dunsmore said she hopes her kids grow up to be just like me, which is a strange thing to say since I am not actually grown up yet and also because she knows that I might never grow up since I have cancer and might die even though I promised Matthew I wouldn't.

While Mom and I ride the elevator down from the children's floor to the lobby, I read a sign on the wall about how there is going to be adaptive ski instruction on Saturday at Massanutten, which is the mountain you can see from the window in the family room. At the bottom of the sign is a phone number and a person's name: Bev Gryth.

"Hey Mom," I say, pointing at the poster. "Is this the same Bev who is a grandmother? Like the one who showed me how to walk with my fake leg?"

Mom looks at the poster.

"Yes it is."

"Well can I go so she could teach me how to ski?"

I expect Mom to say, "We'll have to think about it," but she doesn't.

"I guess . . . you can go," she says. "If Dad is willing to drive you."

I can't believe it! She said yes! I can go skiing! Tomorrow!

Mom has never let us go skiing, since it is expensive and we are saving for college so we can have opportunities in life, and besides, you spend most of your time skiing sitting on the lift anyway. I've been asking her if I could ski for five or six years, and she's always said no, which is why I'm so surprised she said yes today.

Maybe it's because I can't play soccer since I don't have hip muscles to make my fake leg swing fast. I tried to ride a bike once, but I couldn't do it because my balance is different now. And even though I got a hit when I played softball at Lost River, I had to have Tim run for me, which means that I can't really play softball, either. But if I can ski, I will have a sport to play again.

So the drive home from the hospital turns out to be very happy even though we just found out my immune system is tired.

9

If you have the kind of amputation I do that takes off your whole leg, you can't ski with a fake leg on, so at Massanutten I walk on crutches. But with my crutches I can't carry anything so that's why Dad carries my ski for me. He brings it from the rental shop to the bottom of the trails and lays it down on the snow. Then he hands me the warm hat made out of wool. The hat shakes in my hand because I am so excited about skiing. I look up the mountain, see people ski, see how fast they are going. *I* want to ski that fast! I can't wait to ski that fast!

Before we left this morning, Mom said, "Make sure you wear this hat so you don't catch a cold. You know what will happen if you get sick, right?" I said yes. What will happen is I will have to go to the hospital. Whenever I get sick, I have to go to the hospital since I'm on chemo and my body can't make itself get better like a normal body can. Same thing if I get a scrape on my skin. Last summer, the time I tried to ride a bike with one leg, I scratched my leg on the teeth that hold the bike chain. I had to stay in the hospital for three days.

Dad says, "You ready to switch?"

"Uh-huh," I say.

"One, two, three—"

When he gets to three, he lifts the baseball cap off my head, and I pull on the warm wool hat before anyone can look over and see that I am bald. The wool feels scratchy against the skin on my head but at least no one knows I don't have hair.

Bev brings Dad and me over to meet an instructor named Mark Andrews who will teach me to ski. Mark has a gray mustache and is a very nice person because he says he will leave one of his skis at the bottom of the mountain so I can watch him ski on one leg during the lesson.

"Won't your leg get tired?" Dad asks.

"Joshua has to be on one leg the whole time," Mark says. "So I should be able to do it, too, right?"

He is looking at me when he says this, so I nod.

Mark shows me how to stay balanced on my ski by leaning on my outriggers, which are like forearm crutches with ski tips on the end. I wave goodbye to Dad and then Mark and I get on the ski lift. We get to skip the line because he's on the ski patrol.

I've always imagined skis would slide on snow the way my socks did when I used to run down the hall and slide on the kitchen floor when I had two legs. But it turns out that my ski doesn't slide like that. It's much faster. The first time I stand to get off the ski lift, the ski slides on the snow so fast that I fall on my back. The lift—the whole entire lift, which has hundreds of people on it and more people standing in line for it at the bottom—gets turned off when I fall. All these hundreds of people are all looking at me while Mark puts his arms around my waist and picks me up off the snow. I wish I had a microphone so I could say to all of them, "I did not fall because I have one leg. I fell because it is my first time skiing and I thought the ski would slide like my socks used to slide on the kitchen floor."

After Mark helps me stand up, he asks me if I am ready. I tell him I am.

"You see that snow blower over there?" he asks.

"What?"

"The snow blower. The big blue thing right there."

"What's a snow blower?"

"A machine that makes snow . . . We don't get much natural snow in Virginia, you know."

"So this is all fake snow?"

"Yup."

I look around. On the sides of the trail, the snow ends, and you can see grass growing right beside it. The green grass right beside the white snow is kind of like the rubber skin that wrinkles all wrong and rubberlike on the knee of my fake leg— that's the part where, if you look at it, you can figure out it's fake.

"Okay, I want you to ski over to the snow blower," Mark says.

"How?"

"Just lean on your outriggers and let your ski slide."

I am very afraid that I will fall, and my heart is beating fast again. I lean on my outriggers. But nothing happens.

"Push off a little with the riggers," he says.

So I push the outriggers into the snow the way I do when I am taking a step with my crutches. As I start to move, the ski makes a soft noise on the snow like the sound of breathing out through your nose. I notice again how slippery the ski is. It wants to slide down the hill instead of across it to the snow blower. The ski slides more and more down the hill, and I try to stop it by leaning on my outriggers. But that just makes the ski go more the wrong way, and I start to feel my body falling over. As I am falling, my hat gets caught on one of the outriggers. I have to grab the hat with my hand and hold it onto my head so no one will see I am bald.

When I hit the ground—and the fake snow is not soft like real snow is, so it hurts to fall and it knocks the wind out of me so I can't breathe—my ski pops off. I try to catch my breath. I feel sick, like I might throw up, the way I do after chemotherapy. *I wish I hadn't come here today.* I look at the snow and sit still, trying to breathe normally and not cry. *Maybe I just can't play sports anymore.* Mark comes over.

"Let's try again," he says.

When he says this it reminds me of the physical therapist, the one who glued those stickers on my back that made my body bounce up and down. She always used to say things like "let's try this" or "we need to try that." I did not like it when she said these things because *we* weren't going to try anything. *I* was always the one who had to try it. But when Mark says, "Let's try again," I don't mind because he is skiing on one ski just like me. So we are doing it together.

I stand up. He holds the ski in place while I balance on the outriggers and step back into the binding part that holds the ski onto my boot. I push off on my outriggers again and let my ski slide. This time I try to balance my body right above my ski. I'm moving fast enough to feel the air hit my face like wind and to feel my body going faster and faster, the way I used to feel when I was roller-skating down a hill. I slide all the way to the snow blower. I don't fall! I skied faster and faster without falling! Even though I only have one leg! I can ski. I can ski!

"You did it!" Mark says.

I notice that he says "You did it" even though actually *we* did it, together.

The next thing we have to learn how to do is make turns. Mark tells me that making turns is like using the brakes on the bike I used to ride. If you want to go fast you just ski straight down toward the Lift House. That's like pedaling. But if you want to ski slower, you just make bigger turns across the hill. That's like brakes. If you can learn how to put on the brakes by turning, you can ski any part of the mountain, because all ski trails are really the same as this one, it's just that when it's steeper, you make more turns.

Mark says the most important part of turning is where your eyes are looking. "Your body follows your vision," he says.

He teaches me by making turns and having me follow in his track behind him. My eyes follow him, and so does my ski.

Every time Mark skis out in front of me, he adds another turn before he stops to wait for me. The first time, there was one turn, then two, then three, then four. I can't believe that I can make four turns in a row! Then we are back at the Lift House. I smile at the man in the Massanutten jacket. He presses the yellow button and grabs my elbow, and Mark pushes me into the chair again, but I'm not scared this time because I know he will push me right at the exact second the chair is behind my knee.

"How old are you?" Mark asks after we are flying high again.

"Ten."

"My son is eight."

"Oh."

"He's one of the fastest skiers on the mountain."

"Oh, okay."

Finding out about Mark's fast-skiing son makes me wonder why Mark is with me, instead of with him, since it is Saturday, and Saturday is the day that dads play with their sons. But Mark is playing with *me*. It's like I have two dads—my real dad and Mark—for today, and Mark's son doesn't have any dads at all. I guess I got lucky.

By the end of my day of skiing, I don't fall anymore when I get off the lift, and I can ski straight down the hill, right past all the people who thought I fell because I have one leg. I am a faster skier than all of them, and it's the first time I have been fast since last year, when I had two legs and I could run. It's the exact opposite of how I always feel in the hospital when I sit in the children's terrace attached to chemotherapy tubes and look out of the windows that go from the floor to the ceiling so you have a very nice view of the cars and people free to go wherever they want, as fast as they want, seven floors below you on the earth.

I have my second ski lesson a month later. Mark is my instructor again. After he takes me on all the easy trails and I don't fall even once, he says that since none of these runs is challenging for me anymore I am ready to ski the hardest trail on the mountain, which is called a black diamond. I tell him I am not sure I can do it, but he says it is not as hard as it looks from the bottom. So we get on the lift for the black diamond trail.

When we are riding up the ski lift, Mark usually tells me stories about ski patrol. Most of his stories are about people who skied too fast and got hurt.

"You're ready for this trail. You know that, right? But there're always other people on this trail who shouldn't be here," he says. "Once last year when I was out on patrol, a fellow came flying down here with so much speed that he ran right into that snow blower."

"Oh," I say. "Was he all right?"

"No . . . unfortunately he didn't make it."

I am about to ask Mark what it was exactly this fellow didn't make, but then I think maybe he means the fellow got hurt and I would rather not hear about that since I am already very afraid of this trail.

After we get off the lift at the top, I look down at the trail. It is much steeper than it looked at the bottom. It is so steep that it's almost straight down, like a cliff. I am sure I will fall off and die, and at my funeral people will be surprised that I died from skiing, not from cancer, like they thought might happen. But no one will want to say this because they will not want to admit they were expecting me to die from the cancer. When you have cancer, everyone is supposed to act like God is going to heal you and you are going to live, even if that's not what they really think inside. Mom would be mad at me at my funeral because I wasn't careful when I was skiing like she told me to be. And Matthew would be mad, too, because I promised him I wasn't going to die, but then I broke my promise and did it anyway. But while I am thinking about the people at my funeral, Mark says to not be afraid, to just ski like I did on the beginner trail. Just make really big turns.

"Are you sure I can do this?" I ask.

"Definitely."

"Maybe we should ride back down on the lift," I say.

"Trust me, Joshua. I've taught a lot of skiers. You are a natural."

Then he skis away from me, holding his left foot up in the air. He makes a big slow turn across the hill on his one ski and outriggers and then stops. So I take a deep breath and hold it and then I lean forward so my ski starts to slide in the track he's just made, and I follow it all the way to where he is standing.

"See, that wasn't so hard, was it?" he asks.

"No, I guess not," I say.

I make it down the whole black diamond trail without falling or running into any snow blowers and not making it, and Mark tells me I should come back the next week to a race. I have a chemo treatment starting that day, but I ask Mom and Dad if I can please, please, please skip the chemo and go to the race, because I want to win first place. Mom and Dad say no, I can't skip chemotherapy. But I keep asking every fifteen minutes until Mom says she will rschedule the chemo for one day later.

At the race, Mark says that I will be competing in a category called "three-trackers," since I make three tracks in the snow with my two outriggers and one ski.

"How many other three-trackers are there in the race?" I ask.

"You're the only one," he says.

"So . . . who am I racing against?"

"The clock," he says.

The clock? That doesn't make sense! A clock is not a three-tracker, and it doesn't even ski. I can't *believe* this! I spent this whole week, this *whole week*, looking forward to winning today. I even did push-ups to get in shape so I could win. But now . . . there is no one to race against. I can't win first place anymore, because to win first place, someone else always has to get second.

But . . . I guess even if I can't win, I do like skiing fast. Skiing is the only time I get to go fast anymore. So I will still ski today, just for fun.

I ski through the racecourse eight times. Afterward, there is an awards ceremony where Mark gives out medals for each category—blind skiers, skiers with one arm, skiers using wheelchairs, and of course, three-trackers. Since I am the only three-tracker, I get eight gold medals.

After people clap for me, I tell Mom and Dad the eight medals are stupid since I was last place, and they say, no, I was first place, and I say that, no, I was last place, and we keep arguing until an old man walks over and puts his hand on my shoulder.

"Son, I watched you ski today," he says.

"Okay," I say.

"I want to tell you something."

"Okay."

He looks at Mom and Dad, and then back at me.

"I used to coach the United States Paralympic ski team. Have you ever heard of that?"

"No, sir," I say.

"The Paralympics is the Olympics for people with disabilities," he says. "Ski racing is one of the sports in the Paralympics. Like I said, I saw you ski today, and I want you to know that you have great potential."

I look down from his face to his jacket, which is shiny and has a zipper down the middle and is red, white, and blue. On his chest, right in the middle, there are three big patches sewn on. They spell USA. The patches are big and white and strong-looking. Then I look down from his jacket to his pants, and I see that they are made out of the same shiny red-white-and-blue material, and they have the same USA patches, just smaller, near the top of the left pant leg.

"Did you—did you get that jacket at the Paralympics?" I ask.

"Yes," he says.

"What about your pants?"

"Yes. And a hat and a few other things, too. Whole uniform, I got there."

From skiing? A uniform? Really? *Could I wear it to church?*

"If I went to the Paralympics to ski race," I ask, "do you think I would get a whole uniform like that?"

"Of course," he says, patting me on the back. "Of course."

Then he winks at me, nods to Mom and Dad, and walks away before I can ask him where I sign up for the Paralympics, because that's what I want to do as soon as I finish chemotherapy.

I will become a ski racer. I will get a Paralympic uniform. And I will wear it to church.

I have my last chemotherapy treatment two months later, almost exactly one year after I started. Right on time. My immune system didn't get really tired like Dr. Dunsmore said it would. In fact, my immune system got tired and delayed my chemo treatments only once in the entire year, which was the time I was sent home and then got to learn how to ski the next day. So I guess if I hadn't been delayed that one time, I wouldn't have gotten to learn how to ski. It's one of those bad things that God uses for good purposes like Dad always talks about.

To celebrate the end of chemo, we have a big party on the playground behind the church where all the people who helped our family by cooking, cleaning, giving me presents, throwing me extra softball pitches, taking Matthew to Purcell Park to make him feel happy, shaving their heads for me, and mowing our lawn for free—they all come to talk about how great it is that I finished. I beat the cancer! I won! High-five!

We all smile and eat a cake that says NO MO' CHEMO and talk about whether my hair will still be brown when it grows back, or if it might be a different color now. I tell people that I hope it doesn't come back red because I don't want red hair, and if it does come back red, I will dye it bright green. Mom hears me say this, and I think she will tell me I am not allowed to have green hair, but instead she laughs louder than she has laughed in a long, long time and hugs me.

After I finish the chemotherapy, my hair grows back. I get invited to be on the national *Children's Miracle Network Hospitals* telethon which broadcasts from Disney World. One night there is a party at the hotel for all the famous people and for the people who operated the cameras and for the kids like me and their families. At the party there are seven different tables with food on them and you are allowed to go back to the tables as many times as you want to get more like the All-U-Can-Eat Country Vegetable Bar at Country Cookin except the food tastes much better and some of it is meat instead of just vegetables.

A lady wearing a fabric banner that says MISS AMERICA asks if I would like to dance with her. I do not know how to dance with a fake leg. But I do not want to say no because I do not want to hurt her feelings. So I do not say anything, and I look back down at my chocolate-covered strawberries.

"I'll dance!" Matthew says.

Miss America smiles.

"Great!" she says.

Matthew takes her hand, and they walk to the part of the room that has a big square of wood on the floor, wood so shiny it almost looks wet, and they dance on it. Everyone in our family—Mom, Dad, Luke, and me—we all sit and watch

Matthew dance, and we are happy because Matthew is happy.

After he gets done dancing with Miss America, Matthew walks up to the stage in between songs and taps the singer of the band on her leg.

"Um—Paul? Paul? Matthew is . . . doing something," Mom says to Dad.

We watch as the singer bends her knees so Matthew can whisper something in her ear. She nods, and he climbs up onstage.

"We have a special request," the singer says into the microphone. "For the 'Y.M.C.A.'"

People cheer.

"Yay!"

"'Y.M.C.A.'!"

I am confused because I don't know what the "Y.M.C.A." is, but Matthew just special-requested it, and he is only eight and I am ten, almost eleven. How does he know a song that I don't know?

Matthew goes up onstage with the band and leads the whole party of hundreds of people in doing a dance where you make letters with your arms spelling out "Y.M.C.A." I did not know we were allowed in our family to dance on stages with Miss America and lead a dance but I am glad Matthew does not get in trouble for this because it seems like he is having the most fun he has ever had.

It's been one year since I finished chemotherapy, and I am at the hospital for the scans I get every three months. Mom and

I are at the front desk, ready to check out and go home. Once we get home and Dr. Dunsmore calls to say there is no cancer we will order pizza—the white dough kind with pepperonis—to celebrate. But the hospital receptionist says, "Oh, there's a note here . . . Dr. Dunsmore wants to see you before you leave."

"Before we leave? Are you sure?" Mom asks.

"Yes, ma'am."

"Usually she just calls after we get home—but the note—she wants to see us now?"

"That's what it says."

A nurse comes out and says they have a room ready for us. So we leave the crowded, noisy waiting area and she leads us to one of the rooms where I had chemotherapy eighteen times in one year, where I spent one hundred nights of my life. I will never spend another night here no matter what this meeting is about, even if it is—could it be? No, no way, not me, not after I've come this far and after so many people have prayed . . . No. I can feel my heart. I can feel it because it is beating so fast.

"I'm going to go to the bathroom," I say to Mom.

"Okay," she says.

I walk on my crutches into the bathroom and urinate, which feels strange because I've hardly ever urinated in a toilet here at the hospital. When I was on chemotherapy I always had to use that jug, with Mom or Dad holding it in front of me.

I stand at the sink and wash my hands, looking at myself in the mirror above the sink. Hair. With gel in it. And eyebrows, real eyebrows, right above my eyes. When I was on chemo, people always said my face looked pale.

I go back to the room and sit on the bed, waiting. Mom is looking at a book, but I can tell she is not really reading it because her eyes aren't moving.

There is a knock on the door as it opens. That's how doctors enter your room. They knock and open the door at the same time.

"Hey guys," says Dr. Dunsmore.

"Hi," Mom says.

This is the part when Mom usually asks Dr. Dunsmore how her kids are doing, and Dr. Dunsmore says they are well. But Mom doesn't ask about Dr. Dunsmore's kids today.

"Sorry to keep you waiting," Dr. Dunsmore says.

She looks at her clipboard and leans her head to the left. Her hair falls to that side. Dr. Dunsmore has blond hair now. When I had cancer it was brown, so she must have dyed it recently. Or maybe she was dying it before, and blond is actually her natural color.

"I wanted to let you know before you leave today—"

This is bad news. If she had good news she would smile and say "Good news," not "I wanted to let you know." This cannot be good news. Well . . . maybe . . . maybe it is not bad or good, it is just . . . news. Something like "I wanted to let you know that . . . I got a new job at a different hospital . . . We are expanding the children's wing next year . . . I've decided to go back to my natural hair color . . ."

"—that we've reviewed your CT scan, and the preliminary results show—"

No, it is bad news. She looks sad. She doesn't want to tell me this news.

"—there are three small spots on your lungs. Two in one, one in the other."

I look down at her shoes, which are red.

"Now, we don't know what the spots are, and there's—there's certainly no reason to think they are cancer yet. But unfortunately they are too small to biopsy right now."

But why else would she be telling us about this before we go home? It must be cancer. It has to be. Cancer. It's back.

"What do we do?" asks Mom.

"Wait. Six weeks. Then come back for another CT scan. If they are bigger, then we operate."

Her shoes are red, shiny red, so they reflect the lights from the ceiling.

"Joshua, do you have any questions for me?"

I don't talk because I know if I talk I might cry, and Dr. Dunsmore has never seen me cry.

"Joshua?"

"No!"

I say it fast so I can close my throat before crying sounds come out. I keep my throat closed until we are alone in the minivan, and then I start crying, wailing uncontrollably.

We get home and I sit on the floor in between the rocking chair and the window in the family room. I curl up on my side and wrap my arms around my leg.

I see Dad's car drive up the block and park on the street in front of the house. He walks up the yard, and then I hear the *pop* of the dead bolt unlocking, and then the knob turns and the door swings. I don't hear Dad put his coat on the coatrack or slide his shoes off. Instead, I hear his footsteps straight through the dining room, across the kitchen floor, and into the family room. Mom is sitting on the couch, and I am curled up behind the rocking chair, staring out the window. This is the window you can look through and see the backside of Massanutten, where I learned to ski. I hear Mom stand up.

"She called me at work," says Dad.

And then I hear a sound like when you take a coat out of your closet, because Dad's coat is brushing against Mom's sweater as they hug.

"She said"—Dad's voice cracks—"she said it might not be cancer," he says. His voice sounds muffled. His face must be pressed against Mom's neck.

Mom doesn't say anything, but I know they are still hugging, because I haven't heard their clothes brush against each other again.

"But when she told me"—Dad's voice cracks again—"she was crying."

And when Dad says that word, "crying," he starts crying himself. His cry is muffled against Mom's neck, but I can still hear it.

"Who? Dr. Dunsmore?" Mom asks.

"Yes," says Dad. "I asked her why she was crying, because she must see so many kids, and she said it was because . . . because Joshua has gotten to be pretty special to her."

I hear the sound of Mom's and Dad's clothes moving, but it is the sound of them hugging tighter, not letting go.

I see another car drive up the street and park behind Dad's

car. Pastor Smuland gets out and walks to the front door.

"How long?" Pastor Smuland asks my parents.

"Six weeks, then another CAT scan," Dad replies.

"No . . . I mean . . . how *long*?" asks Pastor Smuland.

When he says this, he and Dad and Mom leave the room and shut the door so I can't hear them talking anymore.

I keep looking out the window until it gets dark outside. Mom and Dad walk back in and sit on the couch. I turn away from the window and look at them for the first time.

"I am not going to have any more chemo treatments," I say.

"What?" Mom asks.

"I said I'm not having any more chemo."

"What will you do instead?" she asks.

"Not have them," I say.

"What—and just—*die*?" Mom asks.

Dad gives Mom a look.

"We don't know if it's cancer yet," he says.

"Don't know?" I say. "Come on! Dr. Dunsmore was *crying* when she told you."

"Well, your mother is right. If it is cancer, you will need to have more chemotherapy," says Dad.

"Why?"

"Because we want you with us as long—we want you to live, Joshua," says Dad. "We love you."

But Mom and Dad don't understand. Chemo is just too hard,

too terrible. I am not going to go through it again to get rid of the cancer and then have it come back a year later like it did this time.

"I am done with chemo," I say.

"But if it's cancer—" says Dad.

"It's my life."

"We are your parents."

"So?" I say. "You can't make me—"

"Actually, since you are still a minor—"

"I can do whatever I want."

"We can . . . well . . . technically we can . . . *require* you to have treatment," Dad says. As soon as he says this, I can tell from his face that he wishes he hadn't.

"*Require me?* You are going to force me to have chemo?"

"We don't want to do that, Joshua."

"But you would?"

"We would do what's best for you."

"Which is forcing me to have treatment?"

"We love—"

"What, like the police would come and put me in handcuffs and stick an IV in my arm?" I ask. "You would just let them do it, let them drag me away in a wheelchair? Like you did when I had surgery? Just sit there and watch while they hold me down and pull my hands apart and drag me away?"

Mom starts crying when I say this, and seeing her cry makes me want to cry, but I don't cry because I hate Mom and Dad. They want to make me have more chemo while they just sit there on the couch and watch me lose my hair and my eyebrows and the color in my face.

I decide I will wait six weeks. And the day before Mom and Dad are going to make me have more chemotherapy, I will walk to the bank and get my money and then walk to the bus station and go to a place far away like Kansas, or maybe Nana and Papa's house, and I'll use my money to buy food. But at least I won't die in a hospital bed.

After I run away, Mom and Dad will feel bad for making me go on chemotherapy. Pastor Smuland and their friends will all ask, "Why did Joshua run away?" and Mom and Dad will have to say, "Because we tried to make him have another terrible year of chemotherapy treatments even though he didn't want to." And Pastor Smuland and their friends will nod and say, "Yeah, I guess you should've loved him enough to let him do what he wanted, huh?" And Mom and Dad will say, "Yes, we learned our lesson."

It will be hard to live by myself because even though I am eleven now there are a lot of things I still don't know how to do yet, like paying taxes and driving a car. And my friends from church would probably think it is a bad idea for me to run away, but that's because none of them has ever had chemotherapy so they don't know how horrible it is, how tiring it is, how much it ruins your life, how you can't even really call it a "life," because being on chemotherapy is not really the same as being alive.

On Sunday I decide to stay home from church by myself. Mom and Dad say I should come because going to church is important. But I say no and then I do not say anything else even though they say lots of other things about why they want me to go. I can't go to church because the people there shaved their heads for me and brought us casseroles for dinner for a whole year and gave me extra pitches at the softball game. They thought I beat the cancer. They gave me high fives at the No Mo' Chemo party. But it turns out I lost to the cancer. I failed. I failed all these people and I do not want to have to see on their faces how disappointed they are with me.

The days pass slowly. Sometimes I forget about the spots on my lungs for a few minutes. Sometimes I am doing school-work or playing on the computer and I just think thoughts like a normal person would, like "What is the answer to this math problem?" or "I am going to play *Flight Simulator* on the computer." But then I remember these are the last six weeks that I will live at home and I get sad again.

11

After six weeks, I have an X-ray and then go home to wait for the bad news that means I have to run away. But when I listen to Dad talking to Dr. Dunsmore on the phone, I can't tell if it is bad news or good news. And it turns out it is neither, Dad explains to us after his call.

"So what do we do now?" I ask.

"Wait another six weeks."

"Then what—just get more tests?"

Dad nods.

"I don't understand," I ask. "Why haven't they changed?"

"She said she doesn't know."

"But they could still change?"

"Yes."

"Slow-growing cancer, probably," I say.

"We still don't know it's cancer, Joshua," Moms says.

Dr. Dunsmore told us before it is possible the spots might be something that is not cancer, like scar tissue or stuff I breathed in the air. Or maybe it did start out as cancer in my lungs but my immune system killed the cancer and now the spots on the X-rays are just dead cells. But Mom and Dad and even Dr. Dunsmore have all cried about the spots so I know they think it is cancer. Just like I do.

• • •

A few months go by, and I'm still alive and I haven't had to run away yet. Sometimes though I feel like I am dying and it's hard to breathe, and we have to go to the emergency room but we find out there is nothing wrong with me, which is called a panic attack.

I also go to the hospital—but not the emergency room, the regular part of the hospital—to get X-rays every six weeks, and Dad is still the one who picks up the phone when Dr. Dunsmore calls, in case it is Bad News. So far, though, only the Same News. The spots are still there. Not growing. Not getting smaller. Maybe they are cancer. Maybe not. Or maybe they were cancer that my body's immune system fought and killed. We do not know and the only thing we can do is wait.

When I turn thirteen, we are still waiting. The spots haven't changed. Not Good News. But also not Bad News.

Then I get some really good news that is not about my cancer. One Sunday afternoon when we are driving home from church, Mom says, "Joshua, I heard about something you might be interested in."

"What?"

"I think it was called . . . Mountain Cruisers. It's a ski-racing development program at Massanutten."

"Wow! Really? Can I be in it?"

"Yes, Dad and I have talked about it, and you can join this winter . . . *if* you would like."

She looks at Dad and smiles when she says "if."

"Yeah! That would be awesome! Wait. Who will pay for it?"

"We will, as long as you go to the practice every week."

"Awesome, thank you!" I say. I would give Mom a hug, but I am not supposed to take off my seat belt while the car is moving.

"You're welcome," Mom says. Her voice sounds happy. Normally Mom's voice does not sound happy when she is thinking about spending money on something expensive, but skiing is the one expensive thing that Mom and Dad usually seem happy to pay for, which is lucky for me since skiing is the only sport I can play with one leg. And someday, as long as the cancer does not come back, I am going to become so good at skiing that I will get on the Paralympic team and get a USA uniform like that coach who told me I had great potential.

On the first lift ride up the mountain at Mountain Cruisers—it's the same lift I rode with Mark Andrews the very first time I came skiing—I sit beside a boy named Lee.

"How old are you?" I ask him.

"Thirteen. How old are you?"

"Thirteen."

"What school do you go to?"

"I am homeschooled."

"That sucks."

"What do you mean 'that stinks'?"

"Sucks," he corrects me.

But I said "stinks" on purpose because I am not allowed to use the word "sucks."

"So if you are homeschooled, do you have any friends?" he asks.

"Yeah, of course."

"How many?"

"I don't know, a lot."

"Like how many?"

"Maybe twenty-five."

"Well, at my school, there are eight hundred people, and I know almost all of them."

"Wow," I say. "That's a lot of people."

"Do you have a girlfriend?"

"No, I am not allowed to date until I am sixteen."

"What the! Sixteen?"

"Yeah."

"Man, that *really* sucks," he says. "At my school, there are tons of girls who like me. At the last dance, I danced with seven girls."

"You have dances?"

"Yeah, two of them every year."

"And you get to dance with girls?"

"Duh."

I would like to dance with girls. I would also like to meet the *four hundred girls* at his middle school. That would be so awesome.

"But don't you have a lot of homework?" I ask.

Homework is the big problem with going to Public School. Kids at Public School get five or six hours of homework every day. They start working as soon as they get home in the afternoon and don't stop until they go to bed. But Lee says he can just finish his homework during lunch, except on Pizza Day because he likes the pizza.

"What's Pizza Day?" I ask.

He looks at me like I just asked him a stupid question that everyone knows the answer to, like "What are the atoms in a molecule of water?" or something.

"Duh," he says. "It's when we have pizza for lunch."

"You get pizza for lunch?"

"Duh."

"How often?"

"Once a week."

"Is the crust . . . in that pizza . . . white bread or wheat bread?"

"White, duh, the same color as pizza crust always is."

I guess you have never had to eat whole wheat pizza crust.

I think about the things Lee has told me. White-bread pizza once per week! Lunch periods where you can talk to eight hundred friends every day! Dances where you can dance with four hundred girls twice per year! I know that there are bullies and drugs and immorality at Public School, but I could probably avoid all those things. Public School sounds SO MUCH BETTER than what Mom and Dad told me about it. Homeschool is so boring. Like, maybe when I was a little kid it was fun to have so much free time to play outside, but now I am thirteen and want to hang out with hundreds of friends like Lee does.

So I will start asking Mom and Dad if I can go to Public School, and I will keep asking them every fifteen minutes until I get to go there.

12

On my first day of Public School, Dad drops me off forty minutes before class starts because I don't want to be late. If you are late ten times in a semester, you get after-school detention, which is where you have to stay an extra two hours after seventh period. I know this because I read The Student Handbook three times to make sure I knew all the rules at Harrisonburg High School. I know, for example, that students are required to walk on the right side of the hallway on their way to class, kind of like how cars go in the street. And you aren't allowed to cuss. There are many rules that are only for girls—like you aren't allowed to wear tank tops if the strap is thinner than the width of two fingers—but I still read them, too, because it's important to know all the rules.

Arriving early to Public School, like I do on my first day, means you are required to sit in the cafeteria and wait until 7:42 a.m. Then you get twenty minutes to walk from the cafeteria to your locker and from your locker to your class, which starts at 8:02 a.m. To make sure I make it to class on time, I have three pieces of paper in my pockets. Two are in my right shorts pocket, one in my left. In my right pocket, I have a map of the school, so I don't get lost, and a list of my classes, so I know where to go. The third paper, the one in my left pocket, is where I wrote my locker combination. Except I added an extra number at the end so that if any bullies steal the paper from me, they won't be able to open the locker.

I sit and wait in the back of the cafeteria, which is almost totally empty. Most people, I guess, don't come early to Public School. My heart is pounding as fast as it has ever pounded in my life. I can't believe it! I've made it to Public School! This is amazing! I can't wait to meet all the girls and to eat lunch in the cafeteria, where the lunches of white-bread pizza and other wonderful things cost only $2.32, which is a pretty good price for a lunch of one entrée *and* two sides *and* a milk carton.

It took Matt (that's what he prefers to be called now) and me an entire year of begging and arguing to persuade Mom and Dad to let us go to regular school. But we made it out. Matt is starting at a private Christian school. He would rather be at Public School like me, but hey, at least he's not homeschooled anymore. He had to go to a Christian middle school because Mom and Dad didn't feel like he was ready for Public School. They didn't feel like I was ready, either—or maybe more accurately, they didn't feel like *they* were ready for me to be exposed to drugs and bullies and whatnot—but there are so many clubs and activities and classes that are only available at a big Public School. There's so much to see, so much to do. I don't want to miss any of it. That's why the smaller Christian school didn't make sense for my high school goals and Mom and Dad let me go to Public School.

I am so happy and excited to be here at Public School, but I've also never been so afraid of anything in my whole life—except for cancer, of course. I am afraid I might step on someone's foot with my fake leg by accident, and then she'll want to fight me with her knife. I am afraid of what people will think when they find out my leg is fake. That's why I am wearing a pair of shorts so long you can see only my ankles. I don't want anyone to know about my leg. I want them to be friends with me because of me. Like, my personality. Once people know I have one leg, that's always the only thing they want to talk about.

The bell rings—it's called a "tone," actually—and I walk to my locker. I have memorized the combination, so I don't even have to waste time reading it off the paper. I enter it, and the locker pops open. Unzip backpack, notebook out of backpack, backpack in locker. Okay, we are doing good here; 7:44, eighteen minutes to go—and that's when I see him. Shawn. Shawn lives in my neighborhood, and he's friends with the boys who smoke cigarettes—which they would never do if they knew how awful having cancer is.

Shawn raises his eyebrows at me and glances down. He's looking at the locker below mine. Oh, I get it. Must be his locker.

I say excuse me and take one step to the right.

Shawn opens his locker and starts pulling a notepad out of his backpack on the floor. Should I look in that locker? I'm pretty sure students keep their drugs in their lockers. But what do drugs look like? How would I recognize them? Drugs are confusing because when you hear people talk about the Drug Problem in America, sometimes they are talking about smoking drugs, but sometimes they might actually be talking about injecting drugs with a needle, or even breathing drugs into your nose through a straw like people do with wasabi when they are playing Truth or Dare on church youth group retreats. So I have no idea what drugs look like, and if I saw them in Shawn's locker, I am not sure I'd recognize them. But I have to at least take a peek, a quick look.

I step away from the wall of lockers, leaning back on my real foot. I reach my arms up in the air and bend backward a little so it looks like I am stretching. This will give me a clear view inside the locker.

Okay, here we go, don't be afraid. If there is a weapon, it's all right; he has no reason to hurt me. Take a quick look on three. One . . . two . . . three—

I look right in and see that it contains . . . nothing! All I see is his backpack, which he has hung on a hook. And then, as I am peering in, Shawn looks up at me. *Yikes!* I throw my head back toward the ceiling and yawn, making it really clear that I am stretching, looking up and away, *definitely not* looking in your locker, no sirree. *(No need to fight me, Shawn.)* I'm not sure if he buys this. But I really don't need to be afraid anymore, because I didn't see a gun or a knife in there. On the other hand . . . he might have one in his backpack . . . or maybe he has a secret compartment in the bottom of his locker! Of course! A secret compartment!

Oh no—wait—I forgot about the time! I look at my watch: 7:46! Time is running out! Only sixteen minutes left!

I rush to my first class and make it with just thirteen minutes to spare. It's Algebra II, and we spend 108 minutes hearing a teacher talk about really easy things that I learned three years ago. After class, at 10:05, my lunch period starts. This is a very early lunch, but that's all right, because I am going to eat *school cafeteria* food! Today! Finally! I will be eating a hamburger and a side of French fries—I know because I have a calendar hung on the wall at home with the lunch menu for September—and it will be *so good*!

Dad said he and Mom will buy my lunch twice per week, and the other days I can pay for it myself or pack a sandwich from home. Today I buy it with the $2.32 he gave me. After paying the lunch lady, I stand at the front of the cafeteria holding my tray and wondering where to sit. There are so many tables, so many people. Hundreds and hundreds of people. And they all know one another. In fact, it seems like all of them, even the freshmen, already know *who they are going to sit with*, like they planned it out ahead of time. Did they arrange this over the summer? I stand still for nearly a minute, watching the groups of people gather around tables automatically, as if there were some sort of seating chart that I never got a copy of. This definitely wasn't covered in The Sudent Handbook.

It's not as if I don't know anyone in here. In fact, I know the names of all the freshmen, all 306 of them, both first and last names. This is because I borrowed an eighth-grade yearbook from a friend at church and went through and memorized it. I figured this would help me make friends because I would already know everyone before I got to school. And it *has* helped . . . sort of. I just walk down the hallway like "Hey, Gabriella Decker, how was your summer?" and "Dave Conrad, what's up man? Good to see you!"

A few of them seemed to be thinking that they were supposed

to know me, that they had just forgotten my name over the summer or something. They were the ones who said, "Hey there . . . *dude* . . . how was your summer?" And there were a few people who looked at me very strangely and didn't say anything at all. But most of them have been friendly.

Sometimes the yearbook is sort of wrong, though. On the way to Algebra II, I saw a boy named Carroll Hill, whom I recognized from the yearbook.

"Carroll! Carroll Hill!" I shouted. "What's up?"

I raised my hand to give him a high five.

"Ummmm . . . it's CJ," he said.

"Oh, sorry," I said. "I'm Josh."

So basically I've made a lot of friends. That is, except for one boy who I walked by in the science hallway. I don't know his name from the yearbook, so he must be an upperclassman. Anyway, as I walked by him, he stuck out his leg and tripped me. Then he and his friend laughed.

"That'll teach you to try and limp around this school," he said. "You ain't no pimp! So don't try and walk like one!"

I didn't know what to say to him, since I *always* try not to limp when I walk. I do my very best, but it's impossible for me to walk perfectly normal. So I said nothing to the boy who tripped me. I just stood back up and kept walking with a limp.

Fortunately I don't see the boy who tripped me as I look around the cafeteria. But I do see Lee, my friend from Mountain Cruisers! He's sitting in the corner at a table with two other boys. I walk over to him.

"Lee, what's up?" I say.

"Hey, what are you doing here?"

"You convinced me to come," I say. I tell him this because over the summer I read a book called *How to Win Friends and Influence People*, and it said the number one rule for getting people to like you is to make them feel important. I figure it will make Lee feel important to know he was the original reason I wanted to come to Public School.

"Oh, okay," Lee says.

I am hoping he will introduce me to his friends and invite me to sit down. But he doesn't.

"Can I sit with you all?" I ask, eventually.

"Oh, sure, if you want to," Lee says.

I sit down and look at my hamburger. It doesn't look as . . . *tasty* as I thought it would. The meat is a strange color, not normal meat color—definitely not—and the bun is smooshed flat. I take a bite. I can tell immediately, before I even start chewing, that it is by far the worst-tasting hamburger I've ever had in my life. I can't believe it! I've been looking forward to this cafeteria food for *so long*. I spent so many hours reading over the menu at home, imagining how good the food was going to taste, but when I finally make it to school, I chew and swallow this hamburger, feeling like . . . like . . . like I woke up early on December 25 only to find out Christmas had been canceled.

I look around the table. The other two boys have faces I don't recognize, so they must be in an older grade. Why is Lee sitting at a table of just three people even though he knows all eight hundred freshmen? And why are there no girls sitting with him even though he has kissed more girls than any other boy in the whole grade level?

No one at the table talks during the entire twenty-two-minute lunch period.

"See you later, Lee," I say, when I hear the tone.

"Yup, see you," he says.

Then, as I start to walk away, he says, "Hey."

"Yeah?"

"Are you doing Mountain Cruisers again this year?"

"No . . . you?"

"No."

"Yeah . . . I want to learn how to race," I say. "But Mountain Cruisers wasn't a racing program like I thought it would be."

He nods.

"This year," I continue, "I am going to find a real ski-racing team and join it. That's my plan."

Lee nods, speaks. "I can't wait for the winter," he says.

"Me neither."

I walk to my next class, noticing that people walk on both the right *and* left sides of the hallway, a direct violation of The Student Handbook. In fact, the hallway is nothing short of total chaos, no order to it at all. People walk wherever they want, walk and cuss, walk and cuss and wear spaghetti strap tank tops.

After the last class period finishes, I walk outside. Hundreds of students are standing on the sidewalk, gathered in little circles. And just like the tables at lunch, everyone knows exactly which circle to stand in. No student ever switches circles or even talks to anyone from another circle. I look over at the parent pickup curb to see if Mom is there. Not yet. That means, unless I want to be the only person waiting alone, I'm going to need to choose one of these circles to join. But which one? How do you figure out which circle you belong to? That's when I see a circle, no, *the* circle, the circle that includes Samantha Morris, Megan Murphy, Kathryn Saint-Ours, and Diana Stuhmiller, four of the prettiest girls in our grade. In one of the yearbook photos that I studied quite carefully this past summer, these four girls were side by side, on one knee, with pom-poms in their hands. Yes. I have found my circle.

"Hi, Kathryn Saint-Ours, I'm Josh Sundquist," I say. I work my way around the circle introducing myself like this, and the girls smile at me and return my high five. While I'm talking to them, I try to use their names a lot—something else I learned in *How to Win Friends and Influence People*.

Just then, Justin Burchill walks by. I met him earlier.

"What's up, Justin Burchill?" I say.

"Look at the new guy!" he says. "A total *mac*!"

After Mom takes me home, she sits down in the family room in the big blue chair. I follow her into the room, still talking about my day.

" . . . and Spanish class is going to be really easy," I am telling her.

"Really?"

"Yeah, it's all stuff you taught me last year."

When I tell her about the boy who stuck out his leg and tripped me, the bottoms of her eyes turn red and I wish I hadn't told her. So I try to make it sound like it was all, you know, kind of funny, kind of a practical joke that every freshman has to go through on their first day of public high school.

Even though I met everyone in my grade on my first day of school, it turns out there is a big difference between knowing someone's name and being actual friends with them, between being "everyone's friend" and being anyone's friend, like, specifically. The kind of friend who calls you on Friday night about going to the movies or whatever.

Eventually I do make two such friends: Judd and Brady.

So one time I'm with them at a movie theater. As teenagers, obviously we can't afford the concessions at a movie theater. Our hack is to go by a convenience store beforehand and stock up on reasonably priced snacks.

So we're in the parking lot of this movie theater, stuffing our pockets with the little bags of candy and whatnot that we picked up on the way here. And then Brady pulls a two-liter of Coca-Cola Classic out of his shopping bag. I'm all like, really dude? How is that going to fit in anyone's pockets?

But then I think of an idea. I'm wearing shorts. As I always do, even in Colorado in the winter. The only time I wear pants is when I'm skiing.

Judd is wearing sweatpants. I tell him I need his pants. Can he take them off?

"Right here?"

I shrug. "No one's going to see."

So we switch. He puts on my shorts. I put on his sweatpants. Then I take the two-liter and drop it inside the left pant leg. I tie a knot at knee level, holding the bottle in the pant leg, where my thigh would be. I also drop a stack of cups in. *Voilà.*

We walk into the lobby, and I'm thinking, you know, I've beaten the system here. I've concocted the greatest money-saving hack of all time. And then I look down and observe that the two-liter is swinging wildly with every step. Adults are staring—but pretending not to—even more than usual.

I stop in front of the ticket taker. Well, my body stops. The momentum of the two-liter keeps it moving forward, and then it swings back. So now I've got this bottle penduluming back and forth underneath me like a grandfather clock.

I can't help but notice a security guard standing over by the wall. I can tell he wants to say something. After all, what is a movie-theater security guard there for except to enforce the NO OUTSIDE FOOD OR BEVERAGES rule clearly posted on very prominent signs here in the lobby? I mean, let's be honest, this does not at all look like a realistic part of my body. Not just the way it moves—if you watch carefully, you can see the definite imprint of a bottle stretching into the fabric of the sweatpants.

The security guard takes a step forward.

I'm definitely a rule follower, generally only willing to break rules if they are unjust. Like, say, the prices of movie-theater snacks. Completely unfair. So I have no moral problem with smuggling in a soda. But I definitely still have a rule-follower nature that is afraid of getting in trouble, so my breath catches as I wait for the security guard's next move.

But his face kind of falls when he realizes, right around the same time I do, that there's nothing he can really say in this scenario that won't sound incredibly insensitive to a person with a disability. "Excuse me, sir, I noticed there's something wrong . . . well, not that there's anything wrong with you; it's just that the leg . . . the place where your leg would be, I mean . . ."

So the security guard steps back to his original position. I let out the breath I'd been holding. Brady, Judd, and I make it into the theater with celebratory high fives. We sit in the front row.

I reach inside my pants and pull out a two-liter and a stack of red plastic cups. *Um, nothing to see here, people.* I distribute the cups and then start to unscrew the cap on the two-liter. It explodes, and the soda geysers all over my lap.

Something I've noticed is the older you get, the faster time passes. Which I don't like. Other sixteen-year-olds want to get to adulthood as soon as possible. They don't think about how all this is time they'll never get back. They seem to think they'll live forever. Me? I know the truth. I know how fragile life is. I know how precious time is. So it scares me to feel that time accelerating.

The good news is I finally figured out how to become a ski racer. There was a race at Massanutten. Not an everyone-gets-a-ribbon race like I did with Mark Andrews. A real race with winners and losers. So I just walked up to a guy at the start and asked him how I could join the Massanutten race team. He said you just pay some money and sign up. That's it? Seriously?

It's weird how I spent so many years, like, wishing I could get on the path to becoming a Paralympian but not actually doing anything to get on track toward that dream. I guess I was thinking if I wanted it enough, the Paralympics would just fall into my lap or something. But that's only how it works for bad things. Bad things—like, say, cancer—will come find you. Good things, though, require you to find *them*.

Anyway, that's how I find myself in the starting gate of my very first real race at a ski mountain in West Virginia. I go through a mental checklist. Weight forward. Arc the ski. Shoulders level. But above all, just don't fall. These are the basic rules for being a good ski racer, according to my coaches.

I have them memorized, and I reviewed them in my mind probably two hundred times on the drive over to West Virginia last night. I got a ride with another family on the team because today is Sunday and Mom and Dad didn't want to miss church. They didn't want me to miss it, either, but I convinced them of how important it was for me to get the chance to start training and racing if I was going to make the Paralympics. Just this once. I will always go to church after this Sunday, but just for this one race—

"Number forty-two," says a woman with a clipboard like the one Dr. Dunsmore always used to carry around.

"Yes," I say.

She motions me toward the starting gate.

"Ten seconds," says the referee.

I'm going to win this race; I am sure of it. It's not an adaptive race or anything. Everyone else has two legs. Which is why they are going to be all the more impressed when I beat them all in my very first race.

"Five, four . . ."

But it's so cold. Why is this ski suit not windproof?

". . . three, two . . ."

And why is this race suit so tight? I feel—

". . . one . . . Go, racer!"

I kick through the wand and accelerate onto the course.

I run into the first slalom gate, a single plastic pole about six feet high and one inch wide. It bends at the bottom where it is drilled into the snow. Ice, actually. All ice today. The gate hits me square in the face, on my mouth guard. *Thwhap!* It bounces off me and smacks the ice.

In slalom, only your ski has to get around the outside of the gate. Your body can be on the inside of the turn and run into the gate. Which is technically faster because the closer your ski is to the gate, the faster your line is through the course. Ideally, you want to hit the gate on your shin guard.

On the turn around the second gate, my ski skids over the ice, scraping like the volume is turned way up on a radio not tuned to any station. White noise. *Crrrrrrrrr.*

By the time I reach the third gate, I am completely out of control. The snow is so icy you could figure-skate on it. My ski slides out from underneath me, and I am flying. The frozen surface jumps out of the side of the mountain and pounds into my right hip.

I lie there on the snow, and the thought hits me. *I lost. It's over.* I feel cold all over. *I am not a great ski racer after all.*

I fell. I fell! I fell I fell I fell! *Ahhhh!* How could this happen? How did I fall in my first race? I am a great ski racer, destined for international Paralympic glory, and now I am lying on my back on the ice!

Technically, if your skis don't pop off your boots when you fall, you're allowed to get back up and keep racing. But I've noticed this morning that when a skier falls, they usually just ski out of the course and quit the race because, like, what's the point? If you fall and get back up and try to finish, you'll probably get last place.

I look down the hill and see mostly fog. It's warm enough now that what was snow this morning has turned into frozen rain, coating the top of the snow with a thin, slick surface. I can see a dim patch of red far down the course. The finish line. I decide that I have to cross that line. No matter what. No matter how long it takes. No matter how many times I fall. I will just get back up that same number of times.

The ice has melted against my gloves. I push them against the ground and stand up on my ski. I wrap those cold, water-logged gloves around the handles of my outriggers. I take the next gate on the left shoulder. *Thwap!* The gate buzzes through the freezing rain and slaps the snow. Each time I hit a gate, the ice frozen to its plastic shatters like glass confetti.

Then I fall again. But my ski stays on, and I haven't even stopped moving before I get back up. I go through more gates and fall, get up and fall, three more ice-covered gates, get up and fall. On the fifth time I fall, my cheek gets cut on the ice somehow even though I have a face guard on my helmet. The chemicals in the fake snow melt into the blood in my cheek. It stings. I stand up again, go through two more gates, and then I watch as a red line slides underneath my ski and disappears below the window of my goggles.

The parents huddled around the finish area clap for me. It's a muffled clap since they're wearing gloves, like the sound when you shake out a rug. A few tell me I'm a really good skier. *Give me a break. That was terrible.* They are just saying that because I have one leg. Which is kind of insulting.

But still, I did cross the finish line. Just like I told myself I would. And I'm proud of that.

I slide over to the scoreboard, a large whiteboard beside the finish line, to look at my race result. A referee writes my time as two minutes and thirty-six seconds, exactly two minutes slower than the leading time. Which means I was probably only skiing about thirty seconds, and I spent about two minutes falling and getting back up. So it turns out my result wasn't based so much on how fast I'd skied, but on how fast I'd gotten back up.

Public School was awesome. But I have a bigger mountain to tackle now: the Paralympics. I know I can't be good enough to make the team next year, when the Olympics and Paralympics will be in Salt Lake City. But if I train really, really hard, if I give it 100 percent each day and train as much as possible, maybe I can make the team in five years when the Paralympics are in Turino, Italy.

I hear about a program in Winter Park, Colorado—I get a brochure in the mail about it, actually—where the best adaptive ski racers from around the world live and train for the Paralympics. If I want to make the team, I know I need to be there, in Colorado, training with those athletes. So I write letters to request permission from my principal and then the superintendent of schools to graduate high school a semester early so I can move to Colorado and start training full time. They agree.

Persuading Mom and Dad is a little bit more difficult. I'm old enough now to know not to ask every fifteen minutes (asking *too often* can backfire), but I keep bringing it up, and eventually they understand that this is my dream, this is my shot, and as much as they hate to see me leave home earlier than they expected, they support me.

I just have to figure out how to pay for it. Skiing is expensive. I have to cover my living expenses, training, ski equipment, travel to races—everything. I try to get a corporate sponsor, but no one really wants to sponsor someone who gets last place and falls five times in a race. So I write letters. I send out literally hundreds of letters to everyone I know in Harrisonburg. Also, lots of people I don't know; I get a list of local one-percenters and write them, too. And businesses. All the local businesses. I tell them my story. My dream. I tell them I need their help.

And lo and behold, it works. A check arrives in the mail. Then another. And another. Generous donations. Turns out living in a small town can be boring, and it's weird when it feels like everyone knows your business, but there's a good side, too, which is that everyone *cares* about your business and supports that business if it happens to be a dream of going to the Paralympics.

There's also the problem of my body. Not the having-one-leg thing. I'm mostly comfortable with that at this point. No, the problem is I'm too skinny. Ski racing is a sport where more mass equals more momentum, so successful ski racers tend to be bigger people. I'm, well, not very big. I weigh 116 pounds. I'm all skin and bone. And brain. More brain than muscle. Which is how I figure out, with the help of a nutritionist, that with the amount of training I'm doing—getting up before dawn to work out before school and all that—I need to eat more if I want to gain weight. Like, a lot more. Like four thousand calories a day.

After the first semester of my senior year of high school, I say goodbye to everyone and everything I've ever known and move to Winter Park, Colorado, to become a full-time ski racer. Midway through the season, my teammates and I, all of us being aspiring Paralympians, travel to Salt Lake City, Utah, to watch the opening ceremony of the Paralympics. We watch from the very top level of the stadium, jumping up and down, cheering, saying, "That's us in four years" when the US Team marches into the stadium wearing their uniforms.

After the ceremony, I walk down the cement stairs, wet from the light drizzle—crutches, leg, crutches, leg—until I am on the ground level, looking down a tunnel that leads into the stadium. This is where the athletes—the *Paralympians*—walked an hour ago. I think about this. I want to walk there, too. I want to know how it feels. But there is a pair of guards at the end of the tunnel, silhouetted in the light. Do they have guns? Can they arrest me? I hear Mom in my mind, telling me not to risk it—*it will go on your permanent record, you won't get into college, you will work at McDonald's the rest of your life*. But I'm eighteen now. An adult. I can make my own choices. I march through the tunnel and in between the security guards—"Evening, gentlemen"—give them a nod. They nod back. And then I'm on the field, walking the same lap around the stadium that the Paralympians just did.

Turns out, if you're at the Paralympics and you have one leg, everyone just assumes you are one of the competitors.

The rain has stopped, but there are still shallow pools of water everywhere, all of them just beginning to freeze over. The stadium is quiet except for the sound of the Paralympic torch burning a few stories up, making a sound like a flag whipping and waving in a gusty wind. I walk onto the center stage and look at tens of thousands of people, including Mom and Dad, cheering for me. I am wearing a red-white-and-blue uniform.

I think about everything I've done to get here, to make the Paralympic team, about all the times I've been at the gym and I've pushed my leg beyond exhaustion, and about all the hours I've spent reading books about skiing, about how there are days when I wish I were back home with my family, about living in Colorado with teammates I don't really know. I think about all this, and about how it's all worth it now because I am standing in front of this roaring crowd, knowing that I did it. I finished.

"Can I take your picture?"

The question snaps me out of my daydream, and I find myself standing in front of fifty thousand empty seats.

"What?" I say.

"Can I take a picture of you standing on that stage?"

The voice comes from below me, on the ground level, where I see a man wearing a laminated badge around his neck and a plain black baseball cap on his head. A nylon bag is hanging from his shoulder. He holds a camera with both hands.

"Sorry, I'm not competing in the games," I say.

I'm not even supposed to be standing here.

"That's okay," he says, kneeling down so the torch is framed behind me.

"But hopefully I'll be there in 2006," I add. "So . . . um . . . you just want me here like this?"

"That's perfect."

I clench my jaw, squint a little. The pose of a champion.

"Tell you what," he says, shutter clicking. "If you make it in 2006, I will take your picture there, too."

I smile despite my best efforts at jaw clenching and eye squinting. I just can't help it.

"It's a deal," I say. "I'll be there."

In my first two years of ski racing, despite my obsessive training and focus and endless hours in the gym and everything else, I finish last place in the majority of my races.

It's so bad that my coach actually sits me down at one point and tells me I should stop aiming for the Paralympics in Turino, Italy, and instead be focused on the games four years after that in Vancouver, Canada.

"Because you have no chance of making it to Turino," he says. He's a tough guy, this coach. Years ago he got caught in a blizzard while mountain climbing. He lost both legs, and many of his fingers, and part of his nose to frostbite. Then he started ski racing, won ten world championships and a pile of Paralympic medals, and founded the Winter Park adaptive ski team I train with.

"Really, though? No chance *at all*?" I ask.

"I mean maybe one in a million."

"Aha!" I say. "So you're saying there's a chance!"

He clarifies that he's been coaching for a long time and he wants me to have the right expectations.

"Paul, you may have coached for a long time, but you've never coached an athlete like me," I say. I say that, even if the chances are less than 1 percent, even if they are actually one in a million, I can accept those odds because I know I will put in 100 percent effort. And if I do that, I can accept any percentage chance of making the team because I will have no regrets.

My coach shrugged. "Sundquist, you can do whatever you want. It's your life. I'm just letting you know."

It's not that I disagree with his assessment of my odds. I am looking at the same last-place results he is. It's just that I don't want to look back and wonder what if. What if I'd kept my eye on my original finish line of Turino, Italy? What if I'd trained a little harder?

If I don't make the team, fine. As long as I know I did everything I possibly could. That way I don't have to wonder.

I read a lot of books about ski racing. I learn about a ski racer from Europe many years ago who had this motto called "one more thing, one more time."

Yeah, I think. *Exactly.*

That's how I'm training. That's my philosophy.

I write an abbreviation for "one more thing, one more time"— IMTIMT—on the tips of all my skis. So whenever I stop to rest and look down, I see it. When I'm riding the lift and look at my ski tip, I see it.

One more run through the training course when it's the end of the day. One more rep at the gym. One more book about this sport.

In the summer, I live at Mount Hood in Oregon, where you can train on a glacier. You get up at four a.m. and hit the ice before dawn. Once the sun rises, it starts to melt, and the skiing get slushy. It's kind of miserable. But hey. One more thing, one more time. In the winter, I continue to train in Colorado, but I compete all over: Canada, Austria, Switzerland, Italy. I keep doing 1mt1mt.

In Colorado, I share a little apartment with a few teammates. I get up early each morning, when it's still dark outside. I have to let my car warm up for a while before driving, because it's usually below zero. Many days there is snow on the car that needs to be brushed or shoveled off. Anyway, I drive to the mountain and change into my ski gear in our team locker room, a little space downstairs in the ski lodge. In the morning, our coaches set up gates on a training hill. We make laps through the gates. On each run, a coach gives me feedback about how to get better. At lunch, everyone heads inside, where the blood and feeling return to my toes. Ski boots are incredibly tight, and they cut off circulation. When the blood comes back, it feels like thousands of needles poking my foot. Kind of like phantom pain, but in my real foot.

The training day is over. The formal training day, at least, with the team. After everyone else is done for the day, I go back out and ski the rest of the afternoon. I ski through the trees and over the moguls and down the steepest parts of the mountain. All by myself. One more thing, one more time. The lift closes at four p.m. My goal is to get on the chairlift one more time right before four so I can get every possible run in.

After the lift closes, I head into the locker room and wax my skis. It's best to wax skis every day. The more times you melt wax into them, the more of the microscopic pores in the base get filled in, making the skis smooth and fast. After I finish my ski tuning, I go to the gym to lift weights and stretch. By the time I get back to the apartment, it's dark outside. Time to go to bed and get ready to do it all over again.

The only difference in my routine is on Sundays, when I go to an evening church service instead of the gym. So, yes, I still go to church even though Mom and Dad aren't here making me go. But I'm not quite so strict about religious things like they are. I mean, I don't know if it's possible for humans to understand God's plan, or to even understand God in the least bit. Any metaphor, any word we choose to describe whatever force is animating the universe is, at best, just that: a metaphor. But I appreciate being connected to a tradition and a community of others making these feeble human attempts to understand and connect with the divine.

Those four hundred people who responded to my initial fundraising letter donated so generously that the money pays for my training for several years. I'm not good enough at racing to get, you know, corporate sponsorships or anything. But by the time the donations run out, I've started getting paid enough giving motivational speeches to cover my training and racing.

Five years after that epic fail of a race when I fell five times, it's finally here: the season I've been dreaming about, the season I've been aiming for. The year when the Winter Paralympics will take place. The problem is, even though I've moved up in my world ranking, I'm still not, like, winning World Cup races. Honestly, I don't think I have any shot at making the team. But I keep doing one more thing. I want to finish strong. No regrets.

Fortunately my old coach retired. My new coach, Erik, calls me into his office one day after training. I figure he wants to tell me that the Paralympic team has finally been named and I am not on it.

I sit across from Erik at his desk. He tells me he just learned the qualification criteria for making the Paralympics. The top twenty in the United States, he says, will be named to the team.

I nod. Hey, I have done my best. No regrets. I finished. Not quite the way I'd always hoped, but I have finished nonetheless. Just out of curiosity, though, I have to ask.

"What am I ranked?"

"As of this morning, you are number twenty," Erik says.

"Wait—what?"

Erik smiles.

"Do you mean?" I stammer. "Do you mean that if the team was named today, I would be on it?"

"That's right."

"Weird." That's all I say: "weird." It is so unexpected, such a complete shock.

Then I go outside and ski the trees, a steep section with rocks and moguls, and I shred them until halfway down the mountain, when I just fall into the hill and start laughing. All those people! All four hundred people who donated money, and the sponsors who donated equipment, and the people at college who I told I was leaving in the spring semesters to *train for the Paralympics*, which meant I'd graduate college late—and all that mental energy, years of forcing my body to push through the effort and the soreness. Money spent on training. Friday nights spent at the gym. Late-night and early-morning flights across the country and across the Atlantic.

None of it has been in vain.

I made it. I made the team.

But just barely. That's the weird part: somewhere out there today, there's another coach having a very different conversation with another athlete. *Hey, the criteria were announced . . . and you are number twenty-one. So sorry. You missed it by just one spot.*

At some point, I did one more thing, one more time that this other athlete didn't do. Just one little thing. I'll never know which thing it was. But that was the thing that moved me from being number twenty-one to number twenty. That one thing means I'll get a uniform.

I lie there in the woods until the snow begins to melt into the back of my ski jacket and pants.

It takes a few tries before I can call home without crying.

"Hi, Dad," I say.

"Hi, Joshua."

"You know how you've been saving up your frequent-flier miles for your whole life? For, like, a special occasion?" I ask.

"Yes, mmm-hmm."

"I was thinking you might want to use them next month."

"Oh, really?"

"Yep."

"What for?"

"To go on a trip to Europe."

"Why Europe?"

"I thought you might want to go to Italy."

There is a long pause.

"To Turino, Italy?" Dad asks.

"Yeah. Turino, Italy," I say.

I've been here before, thousands of times, in my mind. Ever since I stood in that empty stadium four years ago, I've been traveling ahead to come to this place, this stadium, to see it packed with people, as it is now, to hear it reverberating with applause, as it is now. And every time I've imagined being here, I've worn a uniform, just as I do now.

We reach the end of the tunnel so that the light from the stadium pours into our eyes as we hear "Stati Uniti d'America!" and the sight of thirty thousand people packed into the arena overwhelms us.

We walk down the center stage of the arena, the United States Paralympic Team. Just like I imagined four years ago. I wonder if that photographer is here.

As we march around the arena and I get a closer view of the crowd, I notice how many of the people have disabilities themselves. I wonder if maybe after the ceremonies a few will sneak onto this stage, get their picture taken. Maybe they'll start training and make it to Vancouver in 2010. They'll be the next link in this chain of inspiration, this chain of hope, that I'm now a part of.

• • •

My slalom race happens on the last day of the games. That night we sit at a table in a little Italian restaurant outside the Paralympic Village, where I am living with the other athletes.

"To drink?" our waiter asks in slightly accented English.

"A glass of red wine, please," I say.

I'm twenty-one, after all.

"That sounds nice, Giovanni," Dad says, glancing at our waiter's name tag. "I'll have a glass as well."

I look at Dad. *Wine? Dad, drinking wine?*

The waiter comes back with two wine goblets and a glass of water for Mom.

"Grazie," I say, feeling very Italian.

Dad and I order a pizza.

"And for you, madam?"

"I'll just have a slice of their pizza," says Mom.

Pizza? Mom? What's going on with my parents today?

"And also a side salad, please," she says.

There it is.

We talk about my slalom race this morning. I tell Mom and Dad what it's like to be standing in that ski gate, a television camera inches from your face, the timekeeper counting down the last five seconds before the most important race of your life. You try to keep your mind clear. Don't focus on technique. Don't worry about falling. Just think about that red line at the bottom, about getting there as fast as you possibly can.

And then you push off—*this is my moment*—and fly down the course, barely able to stay ahead of the gates, trying to push as close as you can to the edge of that cliff without flying off it and crashing. You barely make it across the finish line, and when you slow down, the wind stops blowing in your helmet and you can hear the crowd screaming. *Four thousand people.* If you end with a big slow arc in front of the stands in the finish arena, pumping your fist in the air, a wave of applause will follow you across the spectator stands. It's magic.

But I don't tell Mom and Dad about the next part, when you turn around and look at the giant video scoreboard, praying that it will be like you imagined it, like it is in the movies, a Cinderella story. Instead, you see your name next to 34TH. Which is, like, embarrassing. All these years of training and I still end up thirty spots away from a medal.

That said, for the last couple of years of training, I never really thought I would make it here. I just wanted to give it my best shot. Do one more thing, one more time. Be able to look back without regrets, even if (when?) I didn't make the team. But, as it turns out, I did make it. So I'm not so much expecting to win medals (or disappointed I didn't) as I am just happy to be here. Still alive. At the Paralympics. With my family. Matt couldn't make it, but that's because he's at Harvard now and couldn't take off school, and Mom and Dad thought Luke was too young for such a big trip. Winning medals would be great and all, but if you look around, you realize just being here is the real victory.

The pizza arrives at our table.

"Hey, I have something for you guys," I say, reaching into my backpack. "Some gifts. Here."

I hand Mom a US Team coat. It's white, cut straight and slim in the sleeves. And I give Dad a blue polyester warm-up jacket that zips up the front.

"No, I can't take this," Mom says, stuffing it into the backpack I've just pulled it out of.

Many people say things like this only to be polite. Not Mom. She's totally serious.

"You have to," I say. "I'm not taking it back."

I toss it in her lap.

"Why would you give us part of your uniform? You worked so hard for it!"

"You all are the reason I got here. This is as much your victory as it is mine."

"Maybe I could just borrow it for a few days and then return it?"

"No, Mom, keep it. Besides, I'm giving almost everything away. I want to mail a piece of my uniform or a souvenir or something from here to everyone back home who's ever helped me or donated money to my training."

After dinner, walking back to the Village, we run into Erik, the new Winter Park Disabled Ski Team coach. I've already decided that I am going to give him my US Team vest.

"Can you please take a photo of us, Erik?" Dad asks.

"Absolutely."

I put my arms around Mom and Dad, standing with the sun setting behind us, a pink sky behind the treeless, snow-covered Alps. We are all three wearing some part of my uniform.

We say our thanks and goodbyes to Erik and continue walking.

"You've come a long way since you were nine years old," Dad says.

"I think we all have," I say.

Dad nods. "You know, we've never really told you this, but you almost didn't make it."

"What are you talking about?"

Dad tells me that the day the spots showed up on my lungs, one year after I had finished chemo, when Dr. Dunsmore called him and cried on the phone, she said I probably had only three to six months to live. And that Sunday, the day I skipped church because I was too ashamed of the apparent relapse, Pastor Smuland scrapped the sermon he had prepared and told the entire congregation my prognosis. Then he preached a sermon to prepare everyone for my passing.

What happened to those spots? Nothing. They're still there. Maybe it was cancer, after all, that my body had fought off. Who knows? Dr. Dunsmore can't say for sure. But Dad—who never got to go to seminary but, as an accountant, did eventually become Pastor of Finance at a big church—is sure the spots represent some kind of miracle. And I guess he's right. Not so much the spots themselves, but, like, everything. That I survived the cancer and made it to the Paralympics and my parents got to come watch. It's all a miracle: being alive, being here.

A couple of years after the Paralympics, I find out about a new adaptive sport called amputee soccer. Everyone plays the sport with one leg, on crutches. Turns out there's a US National

Amputee Soccer Team. They compete against national teams. There's a World Cup tournament every four years.

I train. I make the team.

So it turns out I get to be on a travel soccer team after all. We don't travel to play against other cities and counties. We travel to other countries and compete against other nations. Our uniform isn't lime green, the color I wanted so much to wear as a child. Our uniform has red and white and blue and a little patch that says USA.

I didn't end up getting the uniform I originally set out to wear. I got one that's even better.

ACKNOWLEDGMENTS

This is firstly a story about my family, and thus I am indebted to them not only for so freely allowing me to share intimate details of our history, but for the part each member has played in creating the story itself.

I am grateful for the boundless love my parents and siblings, Matt, Luke, and Anna, have poured into my life.

My relationship with the Friedrich Agency began with the first edition of this book over a decade ago. Thanks to Paul Cirone, who represented that title, and to Lucy Carson, who has been my agent ever since and is the reason this young readers version now exists. I'm so fortunate to have such a smart, thorough, and forthright guide as Lucy. Thanks to Heather Carr and the others at the agency who, over the years, have believed in and supported me, especially Molly Friedrich.

Thanks to Ken Wright, publisher at Viking Children's, for his immediate enthusiasm for the idea to adapt my story for young readers. Best of luck in your retirement, Ken. Thanks to Tamar Brazis for picking up the mantle. Much gratitude is due to Claire Tattersfield, my wonderful editor, for overseeing each stage of this project and offering thoughtful feedback that improved it significantly.

Thanks to Opal Roengchai for the lovely cover design. A

special acknowledgment should always be given to copyeditors, including Alicia Lea, Marinda Valenti, Sola Akinlana, Krista Ahlberg, and Rachel Skelton, whose task was especially tricky in this book, where the voice required so many nuanced choices regarding sentence structure and punctuation.

I appreciate both the marketing and publicity teams for working hard to get the word out about this book: Shanta Newlin, Lathea Mondesir, Emily Romero, Carmela Iaria, Christina Colangelo, and Alex Garber. I would be remiss if I didn't offer a special mention of the sales team, whose behind-the-scenes efforts the book industry would not exist without: Amanda Close, Mark Santella, Mary Mcgrath, Todd Jones, Enid Chaban, Joe English, Sarah Williams, and Stacy Berenbaum. Finally, thanks to Cherisse Landau and the rest of the production team.

I also need to shout out the individuals behind the first edition of this book, in particular the brilliant Josh Kendall for giving me the chance to tell my story. Thanks as well to Maggie Riggs, Wendy Wolf, Carolyn Coleburn, Noirin Lucas, Jenna Dolan, and to the rest of Viking for your passion for this project.

This book is the story of my life, but an abridged version, because to properly acknowledge every individual who made this story possible would fill multiple volumes. But I wish to particularly acknowledge the extraordinary care I received at UVA Children's Hospital. When you are a child, it's difficult to understand people's actions, even when those actions are meant for your own good. Looking back, I know and appreciate that I received nothing short of the best possible care from my entire team of nurses and doctors. Special thanks to Dr. Kim Dunsmore and Dr. Raj Malik, as well as Ginger, Teresa, Pat, Cheryl, Kim, and the CMN crew, including Martha and Robert.

My career as a ski racer would never have happened had it not been for Mark Andrews and Therapeutic Adventures, Sandy and the Massanutten Junior Race Team, the NSCD, NASC, Willy J., and Erik Petersen, as well as sponsorships from Head, Uvex, and American Eagle, and the lodging and love from the Nuttings. Thanks to Linda Tobin for spearheading my fundraising and to the literally hundreds of individuals and businesses who donated money to pay for my early training. Your generosity was and is astonishing. Without it, my journey as a ski racer would have never gotten off the ground. I wish to acknowledge in particular the stunning generosity of both the Sease families, James Rollo, the Montgomerys, the Cupps, Wayne Harper, the Cochrans (and thanks for the bedroom!), the Alvises, the Krauses, Shickel Corporation, the Whittens, the Andersons, Douglas Houff, Bruce Elliott, the Rouses, John Holloran, Tom Sowers, the Parishes, Valley Blox, and the Millers.

I wish to acknowledge my many Winter Park and Paralympic teammates and coaches, all of whom I will never forget, and all of whom will be justified in their inevitable doubts as to whether my short and lackluster skiing career deserves to be recorded in a book.

A number of individuals along the way opened doors so I could pursue ski racing without falling too far behind scholastically. Thank you to Mrs. Reynolds and Dr. Ford for letting me pursue my dream during high school. Thanks to Dr. Clemens, Dr. Holmes, Dr. Szykman, and Dr. Pease for generously allowing me the flexibility to take classes from Colorado and even Italy. Thanks especially to the legendary Sam Sadler at William and Mary. Were it not for your personal intervention to grant me housing on campus, I don't think I would've skied that final year.

Dozens of helpful and smart people read early drafts of the original version of this book. I'm grateful. I'd like to especially acknowledge the constructive criticism of Emily Chau, Bruce Horovitz, Valerie Kibler, Scott Moyers, and Rob "Uncle Wonderful" Rouse, and the encouragement of Clay Clemens, Juanell Teague, and David Kopp.

This edition of *Just Don't Fall* happened because of my streaming series *Best Foot Forward* on Apple TV+. Thanks to the many talented, dedicated, and passionate people at Apple TV+ who made this show possible, especially Dianna Lau and Tara Sorensen. I'm grateful to the hundreds of people who worked on our production, both crew members and cast, in particular my fellow executive producers Matt Fleckenstein, Joel Rice, and Meghan Mathes Jacobs. And I couldn't have hoped for a better "TV Josh" than Logan Marmino. Logan, I look forward to watching you compete in the Paralympics and write your own book someday.

Finally, I would like to acknowledge and appreciate the constant love and support of my partner and lover, Ashley.